The Pond

The Pond

The life of the aquatic plants,
insects, fish, amphibians, reptiles,
mammals, and birds that inhabit
the pond and its surrounding
hillside and swamp.

John G. Samson

Illustrated by Victoria Blanchard

Alfred A. Knopf *New York*

Library of Congress Cataloging in Publication Data

Samson, Jack.
  The pond.

  Bibliography: p.
  Includes index.
  SUMMARY: Describes the interdependency and seasonal changes in the
plant and animal life in and around a pond.
  1. Pond ecology—Juvenile literature. [1. Pond ecology. 2. Ecology] I.
Blanchard, Victoria. II. Title.
QH541.5.P63S35 1979   574.5'2632   78-10437
ISBN 0-394-83714-2
ISBN 0-394-93714-7 lib. bdg

Designed by Jackie Schuman

To Victoria—who knows and loves the pond in all its
moods and seasons.

Contents

Foreword

A lot of so-called nature books for younger readers come across my desk. But very few make it home to Heather and Michael, my nine- and twelve-year-old. They love nature. They love to read about it. But not anthropomorphic nonsense about talking animals that aren't as true-to-life as a stuffed Steiff bear. Or utterly impossible adventure stories laced with Disneyish encounters that could never happen in the wild. Or factual but deadly dull science volumes that are about as readable as those stuffy journals subscribed to by laboratory technicians.

Heather and Michael aren't TV addicts. Half my personal nature library is in my son's room, and the books get heavy use. At least those on shelves within reach of arms shorter than mine. Of course, they want to be entertained when they read. So do you and I. But they want to learn. About the real world, about the way animals actually live. And die. About the things they see on our frequent treks in the New England countryside, things that I can tell them something about. But not enough to satisfy their curiosity.

So Jack Samson's splendid book is going home to Michael. And, in a couple of years, it will be passed on, slightly dog-eared, to his sister. It's beautifully written. It's crammed with so many facts I may eventually claim the copy for a reference book. I wish I had known such a pond as this when I was Heather's and Michael's age. I wish we had such a pond just beyond our doorstep today. Some people are that fortunate. I earnestly hope they appreciate nature's gift, and make use of it. For the rest of us, there's no better substitute than THE POND.

Les Line
Editor, *Audubon* magazine

This is not meant to be a scientific textbook about nature and its creatures. There are many of these.

This also is not a "nature" book in which the author will attribute human traits to wild creatures.

This *is* a book that will attempt to show nature as it is without imposing any irrelevant human value judgments upon it.

Perhaps it is too ambitious a project. Only the reader will know that.

J.S.

Everything lives in circles.

The Earth on which the pond rests, the molecules that make up the atoms, which in turn compose the water—the pond and everything in and about the pond are circular.

Around the life of the aquatic plants, insects, fish, amphibians, reptiles, mammals, and birds that inhabit the pond and its surrounding hillside and swamp, there is the circle of life and death.

There is a waxing and a waning, a swelling and a shrinking, warmth and cold, light and darkness—all circular—returning to where it began.

Each day the sun rises, crosses the sky, and sinks below the western hillside—in the ancient circle it has completed since the giant explosion blew the tiny collection of gaseous atoms called Earth away from the sun millions of years ago to orbit about the great ball of flame. But the apparent circle the sun makes about the Earth each day is really the Earth rotating on its own axis in a twenty-four-hour cycle—bringing a daylight of warmth and a night of coolness to Earth's creatures.

Within that circle of light and dark, heat and cold,

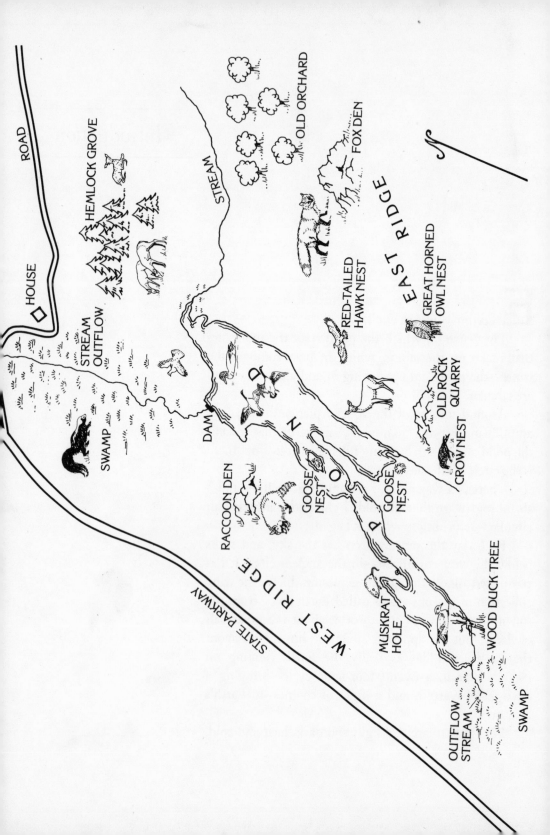

exist the millions of life forms that inhabit this globe upon which rests the pond. And their lives—emerging from the circular egg, or ovum—progress from a beginning to an end—the end producing that which is necessary for the cycle to begin again. And so the circle is again completed and, if completed, which means there is no end—it is simply the continuation of the circle of life.

Of all the forms of life on Earth, only one has looked within—and far without—in an attempt to learn how the circle of life operates, and perhaps more importantly, why? That life form is man. Other creatures follow its inexorable law without question, knowing by instinct that to deviate from the laws which instinct urges is to invite at the least discomfort and at most, death.

So, in the fall of the year, when the spinning Earth's northern axis tilts farther and farther away from the direct rays of the sun and the day's heat warms the creatures for fewer hours than the cold darkness chills them, the creatures react to this age-old instinct. Birds begin to congregate in the northern hemisphere for their migration down the curve of the globe to where the sun's rays strike the Earth for more hours in each day and at a more direct angle. Those that can leave the land of longer and colder nights do so—birds, insects such as butterflies, fish of the ocean, and many mammals travel south. In the spring, when the Earth's axis again begins to shift and the days grow longer and the nights shorter in the northern hemisphere, the creatures begin their migration north again. But the cycle is continued not only in the northern portion of the world, it is also duplicated in the southern half. For the cycle of life is directly reversed in the southern hemisphere—its creatures migrate toward the South Pole while northern creatures move south toward the Equator—in the constant ebb and flow commanded by the spinning globe of the Earth rotating and at the same time revolving in an elliptical orbit around the sun over a period of 365 days.

And during the one-year period of revolving and the rotations of each day of the globe called Earth, its nearness to another globe, the moon, causes the creatures of the Earth to alter many of their daily habits because of the gravitational pull of the moon. The cycle of the intensity of light from the moon causes feeding patterns to change each month as the moon passes closer to the Earth. The gravitational pull exerts an effect upon tides in the seas and estuaries and by doing so affects breeding cycles as well as migration and feeding patterns of all the Earth's creatures—some greatly and some in a smaller measure, but all.

But many of the Earth's creatures cannot migrate north or south as the seasons change. They have had to learn—over millions of years—to adapt or die. Those that have been unable to adapt have ceased to exist on the Earth as life forms and now can be found only as fossils in ancient rock formations. Not only did the giant life forms, such as the dinosaurs, find it impossible to change and adapt to altered climate conditions; so did thousands of smaller creatures, such as birds, mammals, amphibians, reptiles, fish, and insects. They have been gone for millennia, having been replaced by creatures that were able to adapt to the changed climate that followed the great cold of the glacial period in North America and to other global changes.

Many of our present-day creatures show signs of not being able to adapt to conditions and are becoming fewer in number. Often the problem involves an inability to adapt to changes in the habitat caused by man.

Creatures such as the California condor, the Arizona pupfish, and a number of other small fish species find it increasingly difficult to exist in an environment that is constantly being changed by man's increasing population, development, and pollution in its many forms. If these life forms cease to exist, they will be but a tiny entry in the long list of species that have disappeared from this globe over the millions of years because of a failure to adapt.

And who is certain that man, as a species of life, will not disappear too, being unable to adapt? If so, it will not be right or wrong. It will simply be a fact. Among wild creatures there are facts, such as heat and cold, light and dark, need and fulfillment, strength and weakness, fear and bravery, victory and defeat, instinct, intelligence, the cycle of the seasons, and birth and death. There is no *good* or *bad*. There is no cruelty because there is no such concept among other living things—only in man. In nature there is simply fact. It *is*.

The doe will push its fawn of the spring away from the only remaining food buried deep under the snow and eat the food herself. Because survival is what is necessary; instinct tells the doe that she may raise more fawns, but if she dies, the fawn will die too. The doe's survival or fawn's death must preserve, at all costs, the ancient breeding cycle of the deer. A man might come upon the frozen and starved body of the fawn and feel sadness, but to the other wild creatures the death of the fawn simply is a death, and no more. That death may continue the cycle of life for other creatures dependent upon protein in meat form in the cold winter: the fox, the bobcat, raccoon, crow, and any number of other predators and meat eaters.

All these creatures live close to the pond. Many more live in it, on it, and beneath it. The same is true

of the swamp just below the small pond, through which flows a stream, and the woods and sloping hillside above the pond.

The pond is not in a remote wilderness. It is not in Alaska or Canada or a national park. The pond is not more than 300 yards long or 100 yards wide. The 300 acres of land surrounding it are covered by scattered hardwoods, such as a few beech and oak trees. There are spruce trees, and there are softwoods—birch, willow, and elm. A major thruway passes within 50 yards of the swamp, and the noise of the constant traffic to and from a major metropolitan city only a few miles away can be heard at all times. Three houses are built on the hillsides above the pond, and the sound of human voices, music from radios and TV, the barking of dogs, and the clatter of household life echo over the pond during the day and into the night. Two asphalt-covered dirt roads pass through the trees close to the pond, and cars travel them frequently.

Yet within this world exists almost all the life forms that did so a million years ago. These creatures have adapted to man and his changing of the habitat.

To learn about nature and its creatures, and perhaps, with luck, to learn what natural laws govern our entire world, we do not have to travel to faraway places. There is all the knowledge in and about the pond to give us the key to the universe—if we just know how to see it.

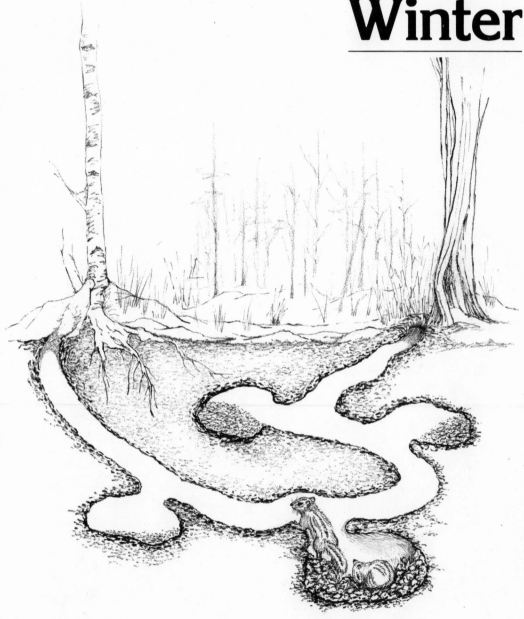

The Beginning

Some say January is the cruelest month of the year in the world of nature.

Almost everything is inert in the grip of cold—especially the reptiles, amphibians, fish, and some of the mammals. But when we speak of cruel in nature we are using a word that applies only to human thought. Cold, snow, ice, and freezing rain are thought of as harsh only by those who observe nature and its wild things. To a painted turtle several feet below the mud at the bottom of a frozen-over lake, the cold is simply a fact. It does not think of it in its hibernation. Its nervous system is controlled by exterior temperature. It will not stir from its winter sleep until that day in the spring when the sun's rays warm the water and surrounding mud to that exact degree of temperature that awakens the turtle to a new year of activity.

Even to the raccoon, which does not fully hibernate but dens up for long periods of time in cold weather, its heartbeat and metabolism slowed down by the cold so that it does not require as much food as in the warmer months, January is simply a fact. It has been simply a fact over the millions of years it took the turtle and the raccoon to evolve into what they are today.

On the surface, January appears to have caused almost all forms of wildlife to vanish. Walking from a road onto the brittle snow of January woods one could imagine the world of nature dead at this time of the year. To the untrained eye there appears to be simply the snow, occasional cold rocks jutting through it, bleak trunks of trees, and the seemingly dead branches of trees and shrubs. Above all, there is either the ice blue cold of a clear January sky or the leaden cold of an overcast one.

There is no visible sign of the many activities taking place beneath the snow, inside hollowed-out logs, within dead trees, inside cocoons, wedged under slabs of bark, or fastened to the tips of twigs. There is no evidence of the sunfish, yellow perch, or black bass that swim slowly in the almost-oil-thick cold water beneath the foot or so of ice coating the small pond. But all are there. All simply wait for the warmth of spring to awaken them or for hunger to become acute enough to make them stir themselves for a short time and seek food.

The raccoon grumbles up from the warmth of a den at the base of a jagged rockpile after it has been hibernating for weeks and heads slowly down the icy slope toward the tiny creek that meanders through the frozen swamp at the head of the pond. It stops occasionally on the way to dig into a rotten log—turning up grubs and other larvae, which it eats greedily. It will catch a field mouse or a shrew in this manner and will eat those just as readily. At the stream it is not difficult for the raccoon to grab tiny sunfish, chubs, and an occasional small trout from the icy water. Or the raccoon can easily find half-dormant crayfish under rocks and can dredge in the sand with its highly specialized front paws until it comes up with freshwater clams.

Having made a meal of these foods, the masked and bushy-tailed animal works its way slowly back to the deep den for days of more sleep. But its tracks in the snow tell the observer not only where it came from and returned but also everything it did while out of the den.

A cold wind moans through the bleak branches of trees whose sap is stored underground in the root system until that eventual climb in temperature sends the sap slowly up the main trunk and into the branches where its fluid will cause the tightly furled buds to open slowly to a world turning green with spring.

In many of the trees the nests of gray squirrels, red squirrels, and the small flying squirrel can be seen. These nests—particularly those of the big gray squirrels—are large, dead-leafy structures that sometimes are mistaken for hawk or owl nests. But hawks and owls build their nests mostly of sticks and generally in the forks of trees, while squirrel nests may be built out on a limb in what would appear to be a precarious spot. It is well built, however, snug inside and—in the case of gray squirrels—lined with dead grass and reeds. The tiny flying squirrel usually finds a den in an unused woodpecker hole and fills it with lining for warmth. Since the flying squirrel is nocturnal, feeding and moving abroad only at dusk, at night, and in the early morning, a beginning nature observer is not likely to see it. Occasionally, however, it lands on the snow and runs for a short distance before taking to another tree trunk, and when it does, its track is distinctive from that of its relative, the red squirrel, in having two parallel lines running alongside its tracks. The lines are caused by loose folds of skin that stretch between the flying squirrel's front and back legs, allowing it to glide between trees for great distances.

Being tree-dwellers, squirrels do not hibernate the way other ground animals do. They are out most of the winter—even in the coldest weather—in search of food. Gray squirrels spend the late summer months and all fall burying nuts in the ground several inches deep and then covering them with earth. After the snow and cold arrive, the squirrel is able to locate these thousands of nuts by scent. Those small scoops of dirt dotting the crust of the January snow are where the gray squirrels dug for food.

Red squirrels, on the other hand, conceal their winter food in underground chambers at the base of trees and among roots. They seldom venture far from these hidden storehouses, and much of their travel in winter to these eating places is through tunnels beneath the snow. The red squirrel will also spend more time around conifers, or pine trees, than do the other squirrels. As a result, red squirrels store cones as well as nuts for food. One can usually spot a red squirrel nest because, if the wood is available, they prefer to line their nests with strips of cedar bark.

January is the month for a lot of squirrel activity other than a search for food. It is the mating season. The male squirrels who live in the trees around the pond spend much time chasing other males away from their territories and searching out females. The young will be born in March.

Under the layer of snow—in logs, crevices, tunnels, and grasses—there are the mice and voles. Active in the winter, these creatures eat seeds and berries they have carefully stored away for the cold months. Even abandoned birds' nests close to the ground may contain several huddled mice nestling deep inside a grassy nest lined with cattail down. The thousands of tiny rodents provide a constant source of winter food for the other predator rodents, such as weasels, and also for skunks, raccoons, shrews, red foxes, bobcats, and winged predators like owls and hawks. The deer mouse, the white-footed mouse, and the rabbit provide the main winter staple for almost all the carnivorous mammals and birds.

Hardly a day goes by that tracks in the snow do not show you where a red fox pounced upon a mouse, or where a raccoon or weasel dug a mouse out from a den or log, or where a great horned owl at night or a goshawk in the daytime killed a mouse on the snow.

Also far beneath the snow, and almost never seen out in the winter, hides that perky little rodent, the chipmunk. It is really a ground squirrel, but its manners and personality put the chipmunk in a class by itself. All summer and early fall these little striped creatures each store about a bushel of nuts, seeds, berries, grain, corn, and flower bulbs in a series of rooms and chambers beneath the ground. The chipmunk's underground home is a master plan of corridors sometimes as long as 30 feet from the main entrance. Along its length are anywhere from three to half a dozen storage caves filled with food for the winter. Beyond the last tiny storage room is a special room to raise the young when they are born in late March or early April. The nursery room is lined with roots and leaves before the female gives birth to the young. Chipmunks even extend their domain to building a large master bedroom and, for the sake of neatness and sanitation, below that a separate room used as a bathroom. The tiny rodents do not completely hibernate, for they have enough food to sustain their life underground all winter. Their body temperature drops just enough to make them languid and sleepy. They will occasionally wake up and reach down below the master bedroom mattress of leaves to dig out food from a special cache. This long, involved

network of tunnels and storage rooms serves the chipmunk well both in the hot summer months and in the cold of winter. For, like some of the other wild creatures, the chipmunk will get drowsy and sleep or aestivate in the cool earth in the heat of long summer days. All this can be learned by digging out a chipmunk's den in the spring or summer. The little animal will soon dig another one anyway. If you leave its food supply intact, it will transfer it to the new lodgings.

Hidden, too, in this deep grip of cold is the muskrat—in a domed cattail mound of a house, its top frozen in the ice of the pond. Inside, a colony of these interesting water rats have dug out a number of chambers from beneath the lodge and have lined them with mud and plants to form platforms. There they will spend the winter munching on the bulbs of water plants, snails, and such food as freshwater clams and crayfish. Like beaver, muskrat dig out a number of tunnels in different directions beneath the lodge leading to piles of food supplies beneath the ice or to holes beneath banks where they can climb out and explore the land. In winter, however, they are subject to attack from owls and foxes if they stray too far from the lodge, so they stay very close to water in January.

Around and near the submerged muskrat house rest sunfish, largemouth black bass, and yellow perch —all moving slowly as they hold themselves upright in the almost freezing water. Occasionally a fish—particularly the larger predator fish—will make a sluggish move and swallow a smaller fish. Because of its greatly slowed metabolic rate, that meal will last the large fish for weeks. In the summer the same fish might eat half a dozen small fish a day to meet food requirements.

Below the muddy bottom of the pond there is no movement. For there lie the banded water snake, the snapping turtle, and the painted, mud, spotted, and musk turtles that inhabit the pond. These creatures are so close to death in January hibernation that it would be difficult to tell if they were alive even by handling them. Snakes, for example, do more than "sleep" in winter hibernation. In true hibernation a snake falls into a deep torpor. Its heartbeat, breathing, and growth are slowed almost to a complete stop. The creature, literally, is barely alive. In true hibernation—especially in reptiles and amphibians and other cold-blooded creatures—the period of hibernation occurs when outside temperatures, which determine the creatures' body temperature, hover between 32 and 40 degrees Fahrenheit. Snakes prefer temperatures between 70 and 90 degrees Fahrenheit. They die if exposed to higher than 90 degrees or to direct sunlight for too long a time, and the lowest temperature they can stand before dying is 32 degrees—the freezing point.

It takes considerable imagination to picture the subterranean world of the water snake and the painted turtle in January. Imagine the complete darkness, clinging mud, and silence of this near-freezing world several feet below the pond bottom. There the reptile and amphibian may remain from the first cold weather in the fall until the spring sun's rays have sufficiently warmed the pond water—and finally penetrated down into the cold mud—to something approaching 70 degrees. Only then, in late April or May or early June, depending on the latitude in the northern hemisphere, does the snake or turtle stir and slowly burrow from its winter grave into the world of light and warmth.

In that stark cold and brightly-lit world of the winter woods, trees, bushes, shrubs, and grasses are not dead. Under the soil and in the root systems life remains. Where do all the insects go in the winter? The easy answer would at first appear to be that they migrate south, like many of the birds. And many insects do. The monarch butterfly, we now know, migrates south to a remote spot in the mountains of Mexico each year. There, in uncounted millions, it clings to trees during the northern winter. But most insects do not migrate. All insects are cold-blooded, which means that their body temperatures are not regulated from within but by their surroundings. Cool weather causes them to be less active, and cold weather—as it does to reptiles and amphibians—brings them to a standstill. Over millions of years insects have adapted so that when cold weather arrives, they stop their body functions and growth until spring. In spring they emerge from resting and hiding places and resume activity. This suspension of life is called *diapause;* in many species it occurs not only in cold weather but also during the extremely dry conditions of drought. The amount of light from the sun, as it moves from longer to shorter days and from warmer to cooler nights in the fall, is thought to regulate this diapause. Insects react to this light by beginning their retreat (or migration, really) into the ground logs, crevices or merely beneath a slab of bark—depending on the needs of the individual species for shelter and warmth. In water many insects travel from above water to shallow water, and others go from shallow water to deep water on their migration from up to down.

Other insects lay their eggs in the fall and then die. The young stay in egg form all winter, then hatch in the spring. Some insects, such as caterpillars, are in what is called the larval stage in the fall. They spin cocoons and spend the winter in them—emerging as adults in the spring. Others simply need some protection as adults to survive the winter.

This vast storage warehouse of food in insect form —along with seeds and berries—sustains the hordes of birds that do not migrate far enough in the winter to escape the snow and cold, or that do not migrate at all. The raptors, birds of prey, such as hawks, eagles, and owls, get their food from killing small game animals and birds.

So, standing in what at first seemed a deserted and frozen forest, a beginning naturalist slowly comes to realize that life is all about him. A soft tapping sound near the crown of a fir tree indicates where a nuthatch is working its way slowly down the trunk of a tree, carefully picking insects from beneath the folds of bark and from other cracks in the wood.

Close by, the soft, high bell-like ringing of a flock of chickadees drifts through the cold air as the tiny black-topped birds search for insects and berries in a stand of spruce trees. Over the brow of the ridge, a gang of crows has discovered a great horned owl perched close to the bole of a huge hemlock tree and has begun to dive-bomb their lifelong enemy. The big owl ducks his head as each crow skims close to his tufted ears, his great yellow eyes blinking in the late afternoon light. The crows will eventually tire of harassing the owl because it is too powerful for them to attack directly. In the long run the owl will win. For the crows must go to roost each night while the owl hunts soundlessly in darkness. And crows are one of the owl's favorite meals.

Stirrings

Even in February, the most frozen-in month of the year in the northern zones, there is life—abundant life. On a day that has several feet of snow, a chilling wind, and a frozen landscape, you can kneel at the base of a tree on a southern slope of a hillside, where the sun strikes the snow, and study springtails.

It is amazing that, of all things, insects are alive and about in the middle of winter. Of course thousands of them are under bark, logs, and leaves, but there are also insects that are carrying on quite an active life in the midst of the snow and cold. A springtail is a tiny, almost microscopic insect. It can be found at the base of trees, especially if the sun has been striking the area for any length of time. Springtails, which are also called "snow fleas," are very active. They get their name from two little "springs" at the end of the abdomen; when the insect is startled, these springs cause it to jump a few inches. Birds such as juncos and other small winter feeders feed on these insects. Springtails subsist on leaf mold, pollen, and various forms of algae. Not only are they found on top of the snow but also on top of frozen water—both salt and fresh. They are hard to see, but if you get down on your hands and knees and take a careful look at what seems to be specks of black powder, you will find the snow flea active during daylight hours.

Another insect that is very active in the middle of winter is the stonefly. The larvae of the stonefly starts feeding and becoming active in the fall and in midwinter, particularly when the sun strikes stream beds where there is clear, fast running water. The adult stonefly crawls up on rocks and mates on the shores—sometimes on snow. The female then lays her eggs in the water. They later develop into the larvae and cling to the undersides of rocks as helagramites. The adults fly about on fairly warm winter days, to the astonishment of the observer, who hardly expected to see a large, bumbling winged insect in the middle of an enviromental wasteland.

The abandoned paper nests of yellow jackets can be spotted in the sparse brush of winter. Open and examine a nest and note the layers of chambers made for pupae or larvae. But don't make the mistake of toying with these cylindrical nests in the spring, summer, or fall—whether they are hung from the limb of a tree or bush or buried inside the hole or den of an animal. The sting of a swarm of angry yellow jackets can be not only painful but deadly. Adult wasps and yellow jackets mate in the fall and burrow into crevices and rotten logs in the winter to await the warmth of spring.

Cocoons may be found on twigs and in the forks of branches and may be the larvae form of caterpillars. Many cocoons are shiny, hard, and porous. They will produce a variety of winged insect species in the spring. Take home a cocoon and place it in a glass jar (section of twig and all) to see what appears. It is wise to punch very small holes in the cover of the jar before

placing it on a windowsill, however. Hundreds of tiny praying mantis young have hatched from one cocoon. An entire house may be filled with these tiny tan-colored creatures, and it takes days to sweep them all outside!

It does not take long to learn how to read animal and bird tracks in the snow. Weasels, shrews, mice of all sorts, mink, and skunks roam the winter woods when hungry. The weasels will hunt constantly for the many mice, which carry on a busy life beneath the snow. The story of life and death is told each day. The mink will stay close to water, and his meanderings can be followed along a stream bed. Both the male and female remain active all winter and stay within a fairly restricted area of several acres. While not the pure killing carnivore that its cousin the weasel is, the mink occasionally will kill mammals as large as a muskrat, particularly when other food gets scarce. For the most part, however, a mink will subsist on small fish, frogs, crayfish, and freshwater clams. It will dig through the mud to get at its hibernation food, especially frogs and turtles. If you follow a meandering stream bed for any length of time, you will discover the tracks of a mink and can tell how it spent its night or early morning hours.

The common skunk doesn't completely hibernate and is fairly active in early and late winter. Skunks do a great deal of digging for food in the winter; much of their diet consists of dried berries, grubs and other insects, mice, voles and shrews, seeds and grains. Following its meandering track in the snow can give you an almost complete picture of its feeding habits while out of the den. After filling up, a skunk will usually semi-hibernate for days or weeks, until hunger pangs drive it again into the open.

At the head of the pond, just where the small stream enters, was the home of a solitary bank beaver. The beaver had been inhabiting the bank den for several years and was past the breeding stage. It had prevented any young beaver from utilizing the pond for building a lodge, possibly because of the scarcity of softwood such as birch and willow in the narrow valley at the head of the pond. Except for the occasional softwood tree cut down in the swamp, the beaver might have gone unnoticed. When a family of beavers is about, there is no mistaking their presence. It takes a great many softwood trees and shrubs to support a pair of beavers, particularly a breeding pair. This pond probably would not have appealed to a young beaver pair because the dam at the end of the pond was man-made: concrete and stone. Water constantly runs over a spillway—more so at peak flow after heavy rains. The runoff forms a small stream, which meanders for about a quarter of a mile down through a swamp filled with skunk cabbage and other swamp plants.

Most young beavers that are planning on setting up a home and raising a family will carefully scout an area until one of the pair finds a site with plenty of softwood trees and a stream with a constant flow that is unlikely to dry up in the dry season. How a beaver determines that a stream will not dry up is one of those mysteries of nature.

After deciding upon a likely site, beavers will start to build a dam. And it is not at any haphazard spot that the dam is built. Through years of dam building—passed down through millions of generations—the animals know exactly where to build it. It will be in a spot where the waters will back up just right and will flood enough softwood trees to provide years of food for a beaver clan. It also will be at the best spot to utilize the

strongest engineering points—the least water pressure and where the dam is least likely to break.

Beavers start out to build a dam by dredging in the bottom of the stream with their front paws. They then begin to weave a complex network of green sticks cut from neighboring trees and bushes. The construction progresses slowly, but at the same time professionally. The pair will sometimes divert the small stream to the side temporarily until they get a particularly difficult section built. The mud adheres to sticks and twigs, and tufts of both green grass and dried grass are shoved into apertures and openings until the dam is a solid mass—letting just enough water through and over it, but not enough to breach it. The tail of a beaver is never used in construction, although a lot of folktales have the beaver using its tail like a trowel to handle mud. The tail is used as a prop when the beaver sits up—particularly when it is cutting trees—and also as a rudder for swimming. And the beaver's tail slaps the water loudly as a warning of danger to other beavers.

Beavers are almost completely nocturnal—particularly around human habitation—although early mountain men and naturalists reported beaver feeding and working during the day in the Rocky Mountain area before men arrived on the scene seeking their pelts. Beavers have few natural enemies, but the few they have are formidable: the coyote, the wolf, the bobcat, the cougar, the golden eagle, and the great horned owl.

The beaver pond, as it backs up more each year, gradually drowns more trees. Most of these are softwoods and provide the beaver with food. But each year the water kills more trees; the pond grows larger and the beavers have to forage farther from the water for food. This means two things: they become more vulnerable to predators, and the food supply becomes more scarce each year. And, when the food supply becomes so scarce it means traveling greater distances overland to cut down trees, the beavers finally abandon the dam and move on to start a new dam in some more fertile area. What they leave behind is a decaying dam, a large area of drowned trees—which eventually fall and rot—all of which results in a rich fertile meadow. Many of the farms that dotted America in colonial days were built on abandoned beaver ponds. This was especially true in the mountain areas of the West, where any flat, fertile mountain land was valuable.

Beavers in the winter are highly vulnerable to predators if they do not store enough cut softwood in food piles beneath the ice of the pond to keep them alive. If they are not able to store enough below the ice, they must crawl from the water and make their way over land to cut and drag trees to the pond.

At our pond there was only the old bachelor beaver. He had felled several trees into the pond to make use of enough food when the ice was thick, and he also had built a mound of branches and bark as a brushpile on the bottom. He was big and old and seemed to have no fear of venturing forth during the cold days to cut fresh food.

Nature's Laws

It is amazing how deer can inhabit a few scant acres of land and almost never be seen.

In winter, the first clue to deer in an area is deer tracks. It is easy to read the tracks of deer, and it will not take you long to differentiate between a yearling, an older buck, or a doe or fawn, although it is easier to tell the difference in a light snowfall. The size of the track as well as the manner in which the deer walks give away size and sex.

On the land surrounding the pond there were approximately twelve deer. To someone walking the land in winter and being able to see nearly across the entire 300 acres it seems inconceivable that the land could support that many deer and yet have them remain almost invisible the entire time. The people who lived in one of the houses bordering the land knew full well how many deer lived nearby. Each spring they lost their vegetable garden to the animals, no matter how high they built a wire fence. The deer still managed to find a way either through or over the fence. Another family, which owned a smaller house on the brow of the hill, did not bother to grow vegetables in the spring and summer but cared more to watch wildlife. They put out bird feeders and food for squirrels, chipmunks, and raccoons. In the spring and summer they put out several salt blocks and were able to watch the does bring the fawns to lick the salt. They were also able to photograph the young buck in velvet and the older buck as late as October when it had shed the velvet from its antlers and polished them up for fighting.

But at this time of the year, March 1, none of the deer carried antlers. It was a lean time. The tips of most of the softwood trees in the forest had been browsed off by the deer, as had much of the grass beneath the snow. The few heavy snows had caused the small deer herd to "yard up" for a few weeks at the head of the swamp, in the thicket of willows where the food was the most abundant. The large buck managed to get most of the food because of his size and strength. So far, two fawns had failed to make it through the winter, and it had not been a particularly severe winter. There had been only three heavy snows—the latest several weeks before and that had melted off on the southern slopes. There was considerable frozen crusted snow on the northern slopes and in the shaded valley. The bucks had dropped their antlers in early January after the rut, or breeding season, and the new nubs were not due to start growing back again until late April or early May. They would become hard again by September, when the velvet was again shed for the mating season.

One of the fawns had simply died of starvation. It was a bit weak to begin with, and nature is unforgiving of the weak. It is nature's way that only the healthy and strong shall survive to carry on the species. When the softwood buds became hard to reach and the snows piled up deep, the weakened fawn simply lay down one afternoon and did not rise again. The doe nosed about

it several times—attempting to make it rise and eat—
but it passed away in its sleep during one of the cold
nights to follow. Its body was covered by drifting snow.
The rest of the deer herd continued to feed in the area
without paying attention to the frozen form beneath
the mound of snow. The dead fawn was eventually
discovered by a foraging raccoon, and in the following
days it was consumed by the raccoon, a skunk, and a
red fox.

The second fawn fell prey to a large black dog
that ran wild in the area and was fond of chasing deer.
Normally the fawn would have been able to outdistance
the dog but the snow was too deep and there had not
been enough food to keep the herd in good shape. The
doe made several unsuccessful attempts to lead the dog
away from the fawn, but the dog was an expert at
chasing fawns in deep snow and kept after the young
deer until it finally ran it down and killed it. It ate
part of it and left the rest, which was finally consumed
by crows and raccoons.

This was not an unusually large number of fawns
for the herd to lose in a year. There were two bucks of
breeding age: the older four-year-old with eight-point
antlers and the three-year-old six-point antlered buck.
Two of the young yearling fawns were bucks, and although they had not mated this recent fall, the chances
were very good they would mate the coming October

or November, when they would be eighteen months old. Some of the doe fawns had mated with the older bucks during the rut in the fall and were due to drop fawns in the spring—about late May or early June. Doe fawns often mate at an age of seven or eight months and produce fawns that next spring. The gestation period for white-tailed deer is about seven months. Not all doe fawns breed the first year, however; some wait until they are approximately eighteen months old before mating—as do buck fawns.

Except for the "yarding up" of deer in heavy snow conditions, the family unit of the white-tailed deer remains fairly small. Although a mature doe may mate every year, she may allow the fawn or fawns of the previous year to remain with her new family throughout the winter. The largest group of deer one could expect to see at any time in the fall and winter would be about five deer. The bucks, except while fighting in the rut, stay by themselves in the cold weather. They keep company with other bucks in the spring and summer, however. It is at this time of the year that the white-tailed deer wears a rugged winter coat that is able to repel the harshest of winds. This winter coat starts to grow about September, and the hairs replace those of the spring and summer coat. When the winter coat has replaced the summer one, the hairs are at first short, fine, and soft. But they rapidly grow in both length and diameter and finally force themselves into a more vertical position and become filled with a very light pith. With this winter coat the deer is able to trap air close to the skin, where it is held by a soft, white layer.

It would be several months before the deer in the woods surrounding the pond began the spring molt. A few months of cold weather still remained.

Two

Spring

4

First Arrivals

It was February 27 and already spring by nature's calendar. On the slope above the pond a red fox was hunting mice in a cluster of dried and brittle stalks of wild raspberry. The male fox would tiptoe slowly through the several inches of crusty snow, its head held high and its nose tilted downward to give it a good view of the matted grasses and tangled brush ahead. When it saw a movement it would suddenly leap high in the air and come down in the same small spot with its two front paws and a wide-open mouth. Most of the time it was unsuccessful, but on one try it reared back after the leap, violently shaking its head sideways and crunching down on the struggling wood mouse. When the mouse's struggles had stopped, the fox dropped it carefully on the snow, then picked it up, and after several grinding crunches of the back teeth, swallowed the warm morsel. Licking its jowls, the fox prepared to begin another stalk when it stopped suddenly and cocked a head upward and to the south. To anything but the ear of a wild creature there was no unusual sound carrying through the woods. A bluejay called from down near the dam and near the head of the pond, a flock of juncos made the area echo with their

light, piping calls; over the hill the sounds of traffic from the interstate highway remained a steady low sound, and several crows called in the distance. But the fox remained staring south.

Suddenly, audible even to human ears, there were several yelping sounds from high in the southern sky—as though dogs were barking far away. The fox shifted its position, rose to all four feet, and cocked a head. The yelping sounds came near and then, in the hard blue of the winter sky, appeared two specks.

The Canada geese, a pair, slowed down their wing-beats and began a glide from several thousand feet in the air while still more than half a mile from the pond. Here, each year for the last seven years, they had nested and raised their young. The fox sat down, its tongue lolling from one side of its mouth. The return of the Canada geese told this animal—as well as it did the people up the valley who looked up and saw the geese—that the long winter was now almost over. It was not a conscious thought in the fox as it was to the humans. Millions of years of instinct told the fox that when the geese arrived to nest, spring had arrived. It would not matter if there were more bitter cold nights and days and even more blizzards and deep snows in the next several weeks. The inexorable law of migration of waterfowl could be counted on to tell the time of year.

Perhaps it was the angle of the sun's rays, perhaps the amount of millilumens of light that entered the retina of the eye of the Canada goose, perhaps the length of daylight and the shortness of night that told it when to start north each year. But whatever the urge, the geese had left the eastern shore of Maryland three days ago. They did not know—and had no way of knowing—whether there would be open water or solid ice on their home pond when they arrived. It did not really matter. A Canada goose can as easily land on the surface of a cornfield in Maryland or the ice of a frozen lake as it can land on open water.

As the two geese lost altitude rapidly—calling loudly as they did so—they slipped sideways in the air, letting air slide from beneath the large primary wing feathers and dropping the tail feathers to slow themselves down—as a pilot drops the flaps of a plane to slow the craft in flight. As they came in over the top of the stark limbs of the trees on the ridge to the south of the pond, they continued to call loudly and at the same time began to drop their legs for a landing. The wildlife in the area suddenly fell silent.

A gray squirrel, digging beneath the snow for the last of the winter's store of nuts, rose on hind legs to look at the sky. A red squirrel, perched on the limb of a spruce, excitedly jerked its tail but did not sound its usual whirring chatter. Even the noisy jay stopped its insistent calling for a moment as the geese set their wings, dropped swiftly in over the trees, and landed on the only open patch of water near the northern edge of the lake. It was a patch about 50 yards long and 20 yards wide where the sun had been able to shine on the thin ice for more hours each day than on the rest of the lake. Still calling loudly, both the bigger gander and the goose spread their webbed feet wide, cupped their huge wings, and skimmed across the ice to skid easily across the dark patch of water to a final halt close to the bank. Both birds, after landing, shook their flight feathers into place, craned their heads looking about the pond for fellow geese, and, finding none, paddled slowly to the bank, where they climbed out and stood resting in the sunlight of the late afternoon. They stopped calling, for it was obvious they were the first geese to arrive at the pond this year. Others would soon follow, but further calling was not necessary.

In the silence that followed the landing of the two huge birds, the older buck deer near the top of the hill lowered its head and continued its pawing for food in the dried grass beneath the snow. The fox shook itself and continued its hunt for mice, and the gray squirrel dropped to all fours and resumed its search for acorns. The red squirrel, for reasons known only to red squirrels, now began a steady chittering sound—perhaps

directed at the geese. The jay returned to scolding a skunk that was digging in a rotten spruce log in the swamp in search of hidden grubs. The female great horned owl, sitting on a clutch of two eggs in the fork of a huge oak far up the slope, swung its large head back from where it had watched the geese arrive and blinked slowly as it settled more deeply on the eggs.

The owl's eggs would hatch in two more weeks—both having been laid several days apart about the middle of February. The furry leg of a cottontail rabbit, partly eaten, jutted out from the sticks at the edge of the nest. The female owl had eaten half the rabbit earlier in the morning, after her mate had brought it on silent wings to the nest just after dawn. She was filled with food and her crop stuck out as a bulge in the breast feathers beneath her beak. Before morning she would be hungry again; the strong digestive juices would have dissolved the rabbit meat, while the fur and bits of bone would have been regurgitated as a pellet—oblong and several inches in length—that would fall to the snow at the base of the tall tree. Pellets are an aid to finding owl nests in February and March, before the leaves hide the nests. Looking for pellets is also a good way to locate hawk nests, but hawks lay eggs later and the young do not hatch until trees are covered with leaves.

The male great horned owl was perched on a heavy limb close to the thick trunk of a red pine down the slope, more than 100 yards from the nest. The crop of the male owl was also filled, and its eyes were closed almost to slits as it perched against the trunk, its mottled coloring making it almost invisible against the bark. It too would not need to eat until the next day, but since it fed only from dusk to just after dawn—

except on overcast days or on very cold winter days when it had difficulty finding food—it would not hunt again until the early hours of the morning. Then it would take a small game animal that ventured out on the snow and came within the owl's incredible night vision and finely tuned hearing. The big owl had killed the cottontail rabbit just before sunrise this morning.

The owl also smelled strongly of skunk musk. Two nights ago, it had sighted a female skunk ambling across the crusty surface of the snow under a three-quarter moon. The sounds of the skunk's meandering walk reached the owl first, and it directed its huge eyes in that direction. Since the skunk had few natural enemies hungry enough to risk the blinding sting and overpowering odor of its scent, it made no effort to be quiet. It had been denned up for four days and was hungry. The urge to make its way to the creek at the head of the swamp, where it would dig for crayfish, freshwater clams, or hibernating frogs, made it careless. Also it was a young skunk, having been born last spring. It had never been attacked by an owl, nor had the adult female skunk taught her young to fear the great predator of the night.

There is almost no way for this fear to be instilled in the young of wild things. Instinct alone makes most small wild creatures venture out quietly at night. Millions of years of being killed and eaten by night predators cause small game animals and birds to move as slowly and as quietly as possible while foraging at night. A flying squirrel or a raccoon moving about at night will move and then stop every few seconds to search the area for the sound or sight of a predator—whether it be a fox, bobcat, or owl. Unfortunately for it, while quick flight will save it from the first two, nothing but a last-second glimpse of the huge owl's shadow will save it from certain death. For owls have a feather structure peculiar to themselves and no other bird: the leading edges of their wings—the first flight feathers—are finely toothed like the jagged teeth of a small saw. These toothed edges silence any noise that might be made by the air rushing over the bird's wing. As a result, owls are able to fly as silently as moths in the darkness—even the great horned owl and the larger great snowy owl of the Arctic, both birds with wing spreads of up to five feet and more.

The ambling skunk never saw, heard, nor had any inkling of its killer. The owl had dropped silently from the top of a dead hemlock—its favorite hunting perch —and its killing glide took it directly the more than 100 yards to the skunk. There was one high-pitched squeal as the huge talons sank into the skunk from where the big owl grasped the animal with its left foot behind the neck and its right in the middle of the back. The skunk released its scent bag full of liquid involuntarily as its body constricted in death throes. The weight of the big bird slammed the skunk deep into the snow; the owl spread its wings wide and convulsively drove its eight needle-sharp, curved talons deep into its victim's body again and again until the skunk finally

shuddered and lay still. Only then did the big owl reach down and, with the sharp beak, cut through the spine just back of the head. Then, carrying the limp and dead body of the skunk as easily as though it had been the body of a mouse, the owl flew with it to a limb close to the nest in the fork of the tall oak. There it ripped and shredded the carcass of the skunk with the beak while holding it with one huge set of claws— two in front and two in back. The female owl left the nest only long enough to waddle out along the limb and snatch a large section of the dismembered skunk from the male. She then hopped back to the nest, where she ripped her portion into smaller pieces and bolted them down—throwing her head back each time she swallowed a chunk.

In cold weather, or when feeding young, the big owls are capable of digesting the equivalent of their own weight in food each day. A pair of great horned owls, in a few months after beginning to raise young, can decimate an area of small game and birds. No living thing—including house cats and small dogs—is safe from these predators. Nature did not teach the owl that a dog or a cat may be a house pet wandering about at night; it is no different from the rest of the small game. If the owl did know there was a difference, it would kill the pet animal just the same. Survival is the principal law by which nature's creatures live, and sentiment plays no part in that law.

So the male owl perched close to the tree trunk and its mate huddled on the thick, stick-entwined nest in the fork of the tall oak. Tomorrow they would kill and eat again, but for today there was only the pleasant sensation of a full crop and stomach, as the late afternoon sun sank toward the top of the ridge to the west.

5

The
Survivors

By the second week of March the snow had melted more on the exposed south hillside sloping down to the pond. But in many areas, especially on the northern hillsides and behind huge trees and boulders, the snow still lay deep and with a hard crust. Since there had been no new snow in several weeks, what had happened weeks ago in the forest surrounding the pond was still there for those who could read the language—perhaps the oldest written story on earth.

At the bottom of the hillside, sloping up to the tip of the south ridge, close to the base of a large beech tree, was the record of the death of the skunk at the talons of the owl. There were telltale signs of other deaths, too, in the old snow. The big owls had killed each day since the death of the skunk, and in some cases the record of those kills was left upon the snow. The owl had caught a muskrat out of the water and about three feet up the bank on the snow. The marks of the long primary flight feathers were left almost four feet apart where the bird had hit its quarry. A few dried spots of blood still colored the snow. And there were the tracks of the water rat leading from the pond but never returning from the disturbed spot where it had met its end.

Its distinctive track—the larger rear feet for swimming and the smaller front feet for holding food—were unmistakable to anyone who could read the sign. In addition, between the tracks there was a line in the snow made by the dragging of the rubberlike, hairless tail of the rodent.

Just below the top of the south ridge, in a patch of snow close to a tall spruce tree, was written the story of the red fox varying its fare from the usual diet of mice and voles. A ruffed grouse had landed on the thin snow near the tree to feed upon some rose hips, dried buds of the wild rose bush. The red fox, according to its paw prints, had seen the bird feeding and had stayed behind a large granite boulder as it crept up to within leaping distance of the feeding bird. The meandering tracks of the grouse showed where the bird had darted in and out of the wild rose bushes until it had circled above the bush and had apparently been feeding with its back to the spot where the fox had finally crouched. There was an area a few yards wide where the fox had landed and slipped in the snow. At the same place there were several wing feathers, and a few yards away, caught in the spines of the wild rose bushes, a number of soft breast feathers of the grouse. Where the bird had taken off were its last two tracks and marks left by the tips of frantically beating wings. The fox had not eaten its prize there; its tracks led off down the hillside from the scene.

Along the edge of the small creek below the dam, where the stream meandered through the frozen hummocks of the swamp, was written another wilderness drama. The tracks of a mink showed in the snow as it had traveled along the bank close to the water. The tracks then left the bank and disappeared. But on a flat stone in the middle of the stream, at the head of a small

pool about a foot deep, were some silver scales, a few
spots of blood, and a piece of fish gills. The scales were
from a carp—fairly small by the size of the scales—
perhaps a fish eight or nine inches long. There were
two other small carp in the pool—facing into the cur-
rent and sluggishly moving their fins in the cold water.
Near them were half a dozen small chubs, some schools
of minnows, and three brook trout. Apparently the
carp was the slowest to move as the mink slipped into
the pool as smoothly as oil being poured. After finish-
ing its meal, the mink had sprung from the rock to
another rock about six feet upstream and then back to
the snow-covered bank—where it continued upstream
until its trail was lost in the rocks just below the dam.

Not all the tracks told of death. There were the
prints of the white-tailed deer as they climbed the still
snow-covered hillside. Near the bases of several spruce
trees the tracks showed where the deer had risen on
their hind legs to feed on spruce tips, the tender ends of
the conifer branches. Not the choicest of deer food, it
was nevertheless life-sustaining at the end of the long

winter. The deer would eat spruce only when much of their customary food of buds from brush and softwood trees had been browsed out. The bucks' prints could be told from those of the does and yearlings, not only by the size but also by the shape and depth they had sunken into the snow.

The tracks of the raccoon, the skunk, and the weasel could be found anywhere from the ridge tops to the edge of the pond. Following the tracks of a weasel always led to kills. A ferocious little creature, it wound its way through brush and stones and along the creeks, killing mice and voles whenever it came upon them. At one point near the head of the lake there was a spot where the weasel had climbed a cedar tree and attacked a red squirrel that apparently had been curled up in an abandoned woodpecker hole lined with cedar bark, grasses, and leaves. The two animals, locked in mortal combat, had fallen from the tree about eight feet to the snow. There they had tussled until the inevitable end: the weasel's triumph. Blood spattered the ground, and the weasel's tracks led off to a jumble of rocks—a dragging mark in the snow indicating where it had pulled the dead body of the red squirrel deep into a crevice in the rocks to feed upon it.

Gray squirrel tracks dotted the forest floor. Each day now, the squirrels scurried across the patches of snow and leaves and dug up the last part of the winter's supply of acorns and other nuts.

The tracks of winter's small snow birds were everywhere—juncos, sparrows, horned larks, grosbeaks, cardinals, jays, purple finches, crossbills, and an occasional robin. Contrary to popular belief, not all robins fly far south for the winter. Some robins migrate down from the far north and prefer to remain in heavily forested or densely grown swampy areas in snowy regions all winter rather than make the long trip to the sunny and warm south. They exist on berries, acorns, and buried and hibernating grubs and insects quite well, and their call can be heard on the coldest winter days. Sometimes a flock of these robins will winter in a small area. They seem to turn a duller gray tinged with olive—and the red of the breast appears to be a russet color in the winter. The red breast will again be noticeable as the southern robins return and the males begin to make themselves shown in the spring —giving rise to the old belief that the robin is the true harbinger of spring.

Mixed in with the ground tracks of other birds were the larger, pigeon-toed prints of the common crow. In March the crow is at its most noisy, quarrelsome, combative, foraging, greedy, busy, and interesting self. In a dense stand of fir trees high on the western ridge and far above the pond was the crows' rookery. It was a quarter of a mile from the nearest house, but even at that distance the inhabitants could hear the noisy clamor of the crows as they arrived at the rookery each evening and left it each dawn. There were perhaps 150 crows in the flock that inhabited the area near the pond for much of the year. They seldom left the region except in extremely cold winters when they flew south in a body—how far no one knew. But, without fail, they were back on the high ridge by mid-March even in the coldest year, and during most winters they remained throughout the cold season.

Showing a remarkable social structure, the flock of crows each day would venture out to forage. Usually they would split into several factions, but occasionally they would all go as a group. Several older crows were obviously the leaders. It was difficult to tell whether they were males or females, for both sexes have the

same black sheen overlaid with a purple and blue cast. But at their calls the other crows would obey instantly —scattering at an alarm call or climbing high into the air at another warning. Some calls caused them to bunch up and fly tightly together—probably as protection against such big predator hawks as the goshawk or possibly a large female cooper's hawk. The flocks would move from the forested area near the pond, and the crows would spend the day searching for food wherever they could locate it. City garbage dumps miles distant were explored and picked over; dead animals killed on the highways by automobiles were eaten; and farms in the area each day were inspected for food sources. When foraging on the ground—whether in the woods or in a field—several sentinel crows were always posted nearby, usually high in a tree or on a fence post. At their first alarm cry the entire flock would take to the air where it would circle until the danger passed or, if it remained, would fly elsewhere.

During this month the crow's main preoccupation seemed to be hunting out owls and hawks. This day they had come upon a big female goshawk that had just killed a bluejay and was busy plucking the breast feathers from it while perched on a limb deep inside the branches of a large spruce. Although fast, the jay had no chance against the lightninglike speed of the biggest of the accipiter, or short-wing, killer hawks. The hawk had banked around two trees—literally on the tail of the fleeing jay—and as the jay dove for the cover of a laurel bush in desperation, the goshawk plucked it from the air with one huge taloned foot. The ground beneath the spruce was dotted with the bright blue feathers of the jay as the slate grey and white hawk with the ferocious red eye, a sign of an adult bird, continued to pluck its meal.

But the goshawk was not far enough inside the shelter of the tree limbs to remain concealed from the crows. The first alarm and gathering call uttered by the crow that discovered her was loud and strident. It was quickly echoed by several other crows, and soon the black marauders were gathering from all over the area. Birds that apparently had been several miles away from the scene when the first calls were sent out now appeared over the ridge tops, flying rapidly toward the spot marked by a number of their brethren already perched in nearby trees. The ones on the scene by now had set up a continuous din of cawing as each bird, from a discreet distance, bowed on its branch and cawed its hate and fear at the big hawk. Frequenting the region only in midwinter, the goshawk had been on its way back to its home in the north country of Canada—feeding on the way. Of all the hawks the goshawk is the greatest threat to crows. Smaller than the slow-flying buteos, such as the red-tailed hawk, the

goshawk nevertheless eats larger songbirds, upland game birds, and small game as the major part of its diet. A good two feet in length, the big female goshawk would have had no trouble in killing and eating a crow.

By now there were at least fifty crows surrounding the tree, and the bravest had begun to dive close to the branch where the hawk continued to pluck the jay. She would pause every few seconds to glare balefully at her tormentors as they deafened her with their cries and dove within a few feet of her. Minutes later, several of the larger and braver crows had flown to branches inside the spruce, a few yards from the hawk, and were screaming their caws literally in the face of their enemy. They knew better than to get within range of the huge, deadly talons, however, and confined their harassment to noise and general hysteria. Finally, tiring of the noise and unable to tear a morsel from the jay without a crow swooping just above her head, the big goshawk suddenly lurched from the spruce tree, still carrying the partly plucked body of the jay, and started gliding down the slope, zigzagging through the forest as she went.

Immediately every crow close to her began the pursuit. The noise in the woods was audible for miles as the black birds followed closely upon the tail of the fleeing hawk. Several more dove at her from above, causing her to alight on a branch of a beech tree close to the shore of the pond, where she continued to clutch the jay and glare at her pursuers. More and more crows began to arrive on the scene. The big hawk was now ducking dives every few seconds as the crows grew more brave at the flight of their enemy.

Finally, deciding that to continue trying to eat her meal was not worth the torture, the goshawk dropped the body of the jay and suddenly launched herself upward and outward from the branch. Executing a half-roll in the air, she made a grab at a startled crow that had just begun its dive at her. The two birds almost met, and there was a puff of black feathers as the goshawk jerked them from the breast of the crow. With a screech of fear the crow climbed for altitude as the rest of the nearby crows scattered in all directions. Landing on another limb, the big hawk ruffled her feathers in anger and disgust at the loss of her meal. Then it dropped from the branch and sped down the valley close to the ground—missing tree trunks by inches and hedgehopping brush. The crows gave chase but it was a token one. They remained high above the trees as they followed in a long ragged line of flight, cawing as they went. The hawk apparently intended to get as far away as possible from the bothersome crows as the sound of the chase continued far into the distance. The crows would at last give up and return to the rookery later in the afternoon.

Quiet returned to the woods—broken only by the soft tapping of a nuthatch as it searched for insects in the bark of a dead hemlock. On the far side of the pond the bell-like calls of a small flock of chickadees echoed across the water as the tiny birds fed upon seed pods.

The ice had melted from the surface of the lake, and the Canada geese—six pairs now—were busy gathering dried grasses and bark strips for nests at various places along the lake shore and on several islands offshore. Others were feeding on a variety of bottom food—tipping end-up in shallow water as they probed the bottom for water-lily bulbs, pond weed, and glasswort. Sedges made up most of their diet when they could find them at this time of the year, but skunk cabbage and grasses would soon form the staple

food. Four of the pairs of geese were adults that had nested at the lake for years. Two pairs were young, in their second year—possibly offspring of some of the other pairs—and had paired up for nesting after arriving at the lake the first week in March.

There had been much establishing of territorial boundaries in the first few weeks of mating and preparing for nesting. The ganders, particularly the older ones, would continuously rush out from the spot chosen for the nest as another goose approached the area. Swimming rapidly and with neck stretched out straight and head held close to the water, the gander would swim directly at the intruder. If that didn't work as a defensive measure, then the big bird would suddenly bugle a challenge and, with wings beating furiously and feet churning up the surface, the gander would drive off the goose precocious enough to enter what the gander considered his territory. After a time most of the geese appeared to honor those lines invisible to all but the birds themselves.

But this afternoon the lake was quiet as most of the geese either fed or built nests. No action broke the surface of the pond. There was no wind and the water had not warmed up sufficiently yet to allow fish to move about. The only movement, except for that caused by feeding geese, was that of a muskrat crouched on a half-submerged rock. It was munching on what was left of a water-lily bulb.

Up the slope from the busy muskrat, the female red fox stopped suddenly in her trot across the dead leaves and swung her head to the side—sniffing the slight air currents. Heavy with the young that would be born in about three weeks, she had foraged from the den beneath the huge pile of rocks far up the slope as much from boredom at being holed-up as from hunger. Moving with her nose close to the ground, she climbed over a fallen pine and sniffed at the still-warm body of the bluejay. She then picked it up carefully and started up the slope. She would devour her unexpected dinner in peace in the den.

6

The Waiting Time

The first days of April came with slashing rain—still cold—but which melted the last patches of snow hidden behind large tree trunks or boulders or wedged in crevices.

To anyone not familiar with nature and its wild creatures, the woods were merely wet, cold, bleak, and deserted. The trunks and branches of the hardwoods glistened slickly in the wet gloom of midday. The uninitiated could imagine that nothing alive was about at this time of the year except an occasional bird calling from a remote area of the forest. But everywhere, if one would merely look, there was life—bursting forth.

In the black mud of the swamp, curling green shoots of skunk cabbage had burst upward as the sun of late March and early April unlocked the cold surface. Buds of all the softwood trees had swollen in the past few weeks and could be seen close up in the lowland areas below the pond. On the exposed slopes facing south even the buds of the hardwoods—the oaks and beeches—were showing the first signs of the sap that was gradually spreading up from the tree trunks and reaching out through the limbs to the tips of the branches.

Beneath the roots of a hemlock, up the slope from the swamp, deep in the subterranean network of tunnels and rooms, a female chipmunk had just given birth to six tiny, pink, furless young that weighed less than an eighth of an ounce each. They were curled up in a nursery room just off one of the pantry storerooms the female had carefully dug. They would nurse for a week before starting to develop fur and their distinctive stripes. It would be another three weeks before their eyes would open and more than another week before they would be weaned and could start on the stored seeds and nuts in the several pantries.

Beneath the great mound of boulders far up on the hillside above the pond, the female red fox would deliver her three young in a matter of days. In the big stick nest also far up the slope, in the fork of the large oak, the two great horned owls were already almost three weeks old. Though they had been left alone, still the size of chicks and covered with a white feathery down, it had been only for short periods of time while the female hunted for food. Now, with the cold rain falling, they were huddled dry and warm beneath the shelter of the female.

And in the relatively shallow water at the south end of the pond, in an area filled with brush, another miracle of birth was taking place. Though the water was still far too cold for the bass and sunfish to start spawning, a female yellow perch had begun laying the first of a string of approximately forty thousand eggs along a cluster of branches. The water temperature had reached 49 degrees thanks to the past few weeks of sunshine. It would need to reach almost to the 70's, and it would be May before the bass and sunfish would start their spawning. As the female perch spewed her eggs along the branches, several male perch swam be-

side her, fertilizing the eggs with milt. The string of eggs would then swell into a gelatinous mass and cling to the branches until the young perch fry hatched in three to four weeks. With luck and a minimum of predation, perhaps a quarter of those eggs would hatch. But only a small fraction of that number would ever reach minnow size, and even fewer maturity. Nevertheless nature, in her wisdom, had provided the lake with enough perch laying and fertilizing eggs to ensure the continuation of the species.

Six young muskrat kittens were bunched together in a warm and dry room at the base of a hemlock root system a few yards down the lake shore. Though the muskrat family had built the lodge out in the shallow lake, about 20 feet from shore, it was used only during the winter and early spring as an eating, cleaning, sleeping, and gathering place for the adult water rats.

In the fall the muskrat had constructed the lodge from bottom mud interlaced with cattail stalks and twigs and branches of softwoods such as birch and willow. Inside the lodge, an upper cave was lined with soft grass and moss. Here the adults had spent most of the winter months eating water-lily bulbs and other food running the gamut from freshwater clams, crayfish, and frogs dug from the pond bottom to an occasional fish. The lodge contained a number of other rooms for sleeping and eating. The one at the top was ventilated so that the rats could breathe in the water when ice and snow locked the lodge in its icy grip. There, while the freezing winds had whipped across the slick ice of the pond and the snows had piled against the lodge and the banks, the muskrat had been snug and full of food. No predator, except a mink or otter, was able to reach them in their frozen house. From the bottom of the lodge a number of tunnels had been dug in the mud, and they radiated in many directions from the lodge to other caves and rooms dug beneath the banks of the pond. There the rats could swim beneath the ice and breathe the fresh air that reached these rooms from small holes above in the bank. A number of other tunnels and passageways were dug from these bank holes and caves so that the muskrat could emerge onto the land if they wished. But—as in the case of the one unfortunate rat that had been caught by the owl while the snow was still on the banks —it was a risk. Foxes were as fond of the water rat's flesh as were the owls, so it was wise to spend as little time on land in the cold weather as possible.

When the ice had melted, as now, the female muskrat moved to snug and well-concealed dens beneath the banks to give birth to young. They had mated a little more than three weeks earlier and would give birth to two more litters before the cold weather set in again next fall. The lodge is never really completely abandoned, even in the hot summer, but it does fall into disuse then. The tunnel entrances are kept open, however, and a rat occasionally climbs into

the chambers, apparently to keep them open. Not until fall do they begin to repair the lodge seriously. Now several muskrat were busy in the rain, lengthening some tunnels that ran along the edge of the lake. These ran through tussocks of dried grass and back under the bank. They served as escape holes and roads in case of danger. Even the mouths of the tunnels leading to the chambers where the young cuddled were reached from tunnels dug into the floor of the pond—in case of low water. When the water dropped the muskrat were extremely vulnerable to hawks, owls, and foxes. Experience had taught them they were really safe only under water.

In a leafy nest in the crotch of a heavy beech limb quite close to the dam, five young gray squirrels stirred restlessly inside the nest. They were almost three weeks old and would be weaned in another week by the female that was curled around them.

The Canada geese were relatively unaffected by the rain. Eight females were sitting on eggs at various places around the pond. A few ganders were feeding in the shallow areas, and others were resting on the banks—some lying down and some with a head beneath a wing—waiting out the rain.

Along the eastern edge of the pond, beneath some heavy foliage overhanging the water, a pair of wood ducks stood on the sphagnum moss of the bank. The female, after days of exploring abandoned woodpecker and squirrel holes in dozens of trees, had de-

cided on a tiny hole in the bole of a beech several yards back from the water's edge. The hole was so small she had to wedge her small body in and out of it. But, after smoothing out the side and the bottom, she had deposited thirteen eggs in a hollow lined with grasses and bark strips. The home of the young wood ducks had been settled upon. Having just fed on water plants, she was readying herself to return to the nest to incubate while the brightly colored male would stand guard over the territory surrounding the tree.

At the base of a huge rock split by a crevass, halfway up a slope to the west of the dam, a female raccoon was nuzzling four kittens born three days ago. The big male with whom she had mated in the first part of February had only hours ago brought her a huge egg on which she had fed hungrily. The Canada goose that had waddled down to the pond to eat for a moment, earlier in the morning, had been slightly puzzled when she returned to the nest to find a space missing in her clutch of eggs. Where there had been five, there were now only three. After turning about several times and moving the remaining eggs with her beak, she had settled on the eggs again. Something vaguely bothered her, but since neither she nor the gander had seen the big boar raccoon creep from the sedges and take the two eggs—one for himself and one for his mate—the goose preened her feathers for a moment and then rested carefully on the three remaining eggs.

7

First Gosling

It was early in the morning of April 26. One of the geese, on a small island just behind a point of land jutting into the pond from the south, stirred and probed beneath herself in the nest. She had heard the first "pipping" sound from one of the five eggs beneath her. The tiny gosling was pecking away at the inside of the egg with the sharp protuberance, or egg tooth, on its bill.

The length of time necessary for a gosling to emerge from the egg varies from several hours to a full day. Also, in Canada geese—as in many other goose species and some ducks—incubation of all the eggs had begun at the same time. Nature over the millions of years had taught the goose that it was far better for all the young to hatch at roughly the same time. That way, young that hatched first and tended to stray from the nest would not be vulnerable to predators while the female was still incubating the rest of the eggs in the clutch. In order to achieve this simultaneous hatching, the goose did not begin sitting on the first or second egg that was laid. She laid as many eggs as she intended to incubate, leaving them uncovered until the next arrived, usually several days apart. After she had laid the last egg, she

lined the nest with grasses and warm down from her body and settled on the eggs. For much of the incubation time—in this case twenty-eight days—the female fasted. Only occasionally did she leave the nest and this only when a warm sun beat down on the eggs. The gander stood guard the entire time to keep all other geese and would-be predators away from the small island.

For five hours—into the middle of the afternoon—the goose shifted uneasily as the gosling pecked away at the confining shell. Finally she suddenly stood up and called to the gander, who was swimming about 30 feet from the island. The gander immediately swam to the rocks at the island edge and clambered up on the flat close to the edge. Both adults watched intently as a gosling finally split the covering of the large egg and struggled out of the cracked shell. The yellow down was wet and the gosling's eyes were open. Unsteady on its small feet, it began wobbling about the nest uttering a faint "peep, peep" as it attempted to crawl beneath the female. No other sounds had been heard from the other eggs. Usually all the goslings began to hatch at roughly the same time, but this did not seem to be of any concern to the geese. Perhaps the other eggs were infertile. Sometimes only two out of six eggs would hatch, or

First Gosling

three out of five. The previous year one nesting pair of geese on an adjoining island had successfully hatched six out of six eggs; another pair, nesting on a point of land less than 100 yards away, had managed to hatch only one gosling out of five eggs.

For twenty minutes the gosling staggered around the nest and the adjoining area while both adults watched carefully. The down on the new gosling was dry and fluffy in the warm sun. The female gently nudged the remaining eggs. Perhaps she felt it might tend to awaken the other young into trying to escape the egg.

Suddenly, after tottering to the edge of the bank near the nest, the gosling lost its footing and tumbled down the steep bank for a few feet—ending in the water. Both adults emitted alarm calls, but only the gander clambered down into the water and began swimming in an arc close to the tiny ball of yellow down that floated on the water as light as a wisp of milkweed. Only a few hours old, the gosling was as at home in the water as on land. Not caring for the temperature of the water, which by now must have reached at least 60 degrees Fahrenheit, the gosling kept up an incessant "peep, peep, peep" as it attempted to find a foothold on the steep dirt and slippery rocks lining the bank. One would think the gander or the goose would simply reach down and pluck the ball of fluff from the water but, as happens in much of nature, they inexplicably seemed to wait for fate to decide the destiny of the gosling.

After an interlude of almost an hour, the gosling finally found a small ravine in the dirt and managed to scramble its way back to the surface of the small island. It then stumbled its way back to the nest and snuggled beneath the goose. Apparently the other goslings had

not yet felt the urge to emerge from the eggs.

As the gosling's peeping sound ceased, a silence fell across the pond, broken only by the raucous clattering call of a kingfisher perched upon a fragile branch of a birch tree above the small stream below the dam. The bird had just dived into a small pool and speared an ironcolor shiner that had been engaged in a spawning race with a number of other minnows in the creek. The breeding season for the minnows had just started—carrying over to September—and they had just taken on the orange breeding color which gives them the name. The kingfisher was well aware of the shiners and had been for several days. The water temperature in the sandy-bottom creek had reached 62 degrees, and the eggs of the minnows would hatch a little more than two days after the adults had bred. The egg sac that would accompany the fry upon hatching would disappear after the fifth day, and the young fish would remain in large schools until they reached a length of almost half an inch and would join the schools of larger shiners. They would, meanwhile, provide a steady source of food for the kingfisher, which was bringing food to a mate incubating eggs eight feet back in a tunnel dug far into a clay bank close to the base of the dam. The mate was sitting on six white eggs in a hollowed-out cave at the end of the tunnel.

And all across the forest area surrounding the pond and in the lowlands near the swamp the trees were beginning to sprout the first bright green unfurlings of leaves. Some were far ahead of others, but all showed the warming of the sun in recent weeks. Over the hill and along the interstate highway the weeping willows had been green for more than a week.

8

Bursting Forth

By May 15 new life in the area of the pond was bursting out everywhere. The trees and shrubs were covered with new green leaves, the swamp was luxuriant with a heavy carpet of skunk cabbage, and the dogwood trees on the western edge of the pond were bursting into bloom.

The baby geese, now several weeks old, were at home on both land and water. The adults had taken them several hundred yards from the pond, and much of the days were now being spent along the small stream below the dam where the young were taught to probe for aquatic plants, bulbs, and water insects in the gravel bottom. The adults, meanwhile, filled up on the leaves of the lush skunk cabbage.

All along the edge of the pond, particularly where there was a sandy bottom, the sunfish and bass were beginning to spawn. The water temperature had reached the high 60's, and the shallow depressions dug by sunfish were everywhere—most in water less than a foot deep and about eight inches in width. The nests were guarded constantly by the male sunfish after the females had laid a great many eggs, which had been fertilized by the males. In many cases the female laid thousands of eggs at one time.

Sunfish eggs are sand-colored and stick to one another and to particles of sand on the bottom of the nest. The young hatch in the warm water after five days, and the male continues to guard them—chasing off all invaders to his territory and gathering the school of newly hatched fry close to the nest at night. They keep this up for two to three weeks until the young finally manage to swim off into areas of aquatic vegetation—those that are not eaten by small predator fish: small sunfish, minnows, perch, and bass.

The largemouth black bass prefer slightly deeper water but also nest over sand. By now, most of the bass had scooped out hollow nests—some as much as 20 inches in diameter—off points of land jutting out into the pond. The scooping out of the nest was done by the male bass, who performed this task by finning away the top covering of mud and silt and in many cases actually picking up bits of gravel and sand in order to deepen and widen the nest.

Most nests are about eight feet from the shoreline and in water about a foot and a half deep. The female bass, heavy with eggs, deposit eggs in several nests along the shoreline. Unlike the sunfish, which tend to nest in colonies, the nests of the bass are more than 20 feet apart. These big, voracious predator fish attempt to chase every other form of life, amphibian or fish, away from the nest. The eggs, which cling to the bottom as do those of the sunfish, are fertilized by the male that digs the nest. The female may return to the same nest to spawn with the same male or she may cover a number of nests while laying her eggs. More than one female bass also may lay eggs in the same nest to be fertilized by the resident male. The females lay a great many eggs—somewhere around fifteen to twenty thousand for a four-pound female.

The males spend all their time defending the eggs, but many eggs fall prey to scavenging small fish such as perch and sunfish. The male becomes harassed as more and more eggs are stolen from the nest by small fish and occasionally by turtles. The more scavengers the male chases away, the more the ever-ready circle of smaller fish tries to reach the eggs.

The eggs hatch into small bass fry in anywhere from a week to ten days, depending upon the water temperature. The higher the temperature, the shorter the incubation period. The fry are hatched with a yoke sac attached and remain on the nest where the male can guard them until the yoke sac has been absorbed—at which time the young form a school and swim off to weedy areas where they feed on plankton and aquatic insects in cover, relatively safe from other predator fish. With luck the small bass grow from two to four inches the first year, and by the time the bass are two years old they should be from five to seven inches long.

One bass of about three pounds had been busy chasing off small fish from his nest for hours when suddenly a small musk turtle swam in from the weeds and began to eat eggs. The bass charged up to the turtle and nosed it gradually back from the nest until it was a few feet away. The turtle pulled in its head and feet when the bass came close to it and stayed that way while the bass eased it gradually away from the nest. When the bass had pushed the hungry turtle—which was about three inches in diameter—to what it considered a safe distance, it swam back to the nest to continue chasing away the small fish.

As soon as the bass left, the small turtle poked its head and legs from the shell and rapidly swam back to the nest to continue feeding. The harried bass repeated the performance at least five times, and each time the turtle returned. Finally the bass simply opened its huge mouth, picked up the turtle, and swam as rapidly as it could up the lake shore for a distance of about 30 yards. There it suddenly spat out the annoying turtle in shallow water and sped back to its nest. The turtle —apparently disoriented by its quick trip—regained its equilibrium finally and swam off into deep water.

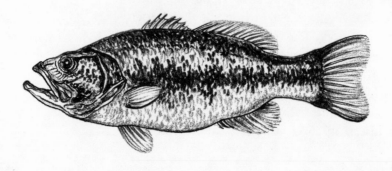

The warm sun beat down on the pond and its surroundings. At the head of the pond, where the water
was very shallow and the area was overgrown with
grasses and sedges, some dead tree trunks jutted out and
a few drowned bushes stuck up through the surface at
the edge of the shore. There the spring peepers were
singing their spring breeding song. The series of hundreds of "peeps" blended into a continuous level of
sound until it sounded a bit like the summer song of
cicadas or locusts. Literally hundreds of these tiny
treefrogs were clinging to grass stems, dead vegetation,
and twigs.

Others floated in the water, some united in breeding. And at the neck of each tiny singer was an in-
flated air sac as the little frogs sang. It matters little
how experienced a naturalist may be, it is almost
impossible to see these little harbingers of spring in the
daylight. As soon as anything approaches—human, a
marauding raccoon, a stalking green heron, a swimming muskrat—the peepers fall silent. So well are they
camouflaged that they are almost impossible to spot.
Only at night can you hope to capture or photograph
these little spring songsters. They completely ignore a
flashlight—perhaps mistaking it for the moon—and will
continue to sing even when the light is lowered to
within a few inches of them.

The peepers were not the only frogs active in the
warm sun. Green frogs sang from the lily pads and
duckweed in the shallows—their call sounding much
like a breaking banjo string. Leopard frogs, some in
the water and others in the sprouting ferns and sphagnum moss of the bank and swamp, let the world know
they were alive in the breeding season with their calls
that sounded like a rattling snore interrupted by a
series of grunts. Gray treefrogs, some in trees but far

more in the lower brush surrounding the lake, filled the lake with their calls—a high, continuous trilling sound. And somewhere along the western edge of the pond, deep in a cove filled with water lilies, came the resonant, booming call of a single bullfrog.

Only one species of snake had come out of winter hibernation. The rest of the native species of snakes that lived in the terrain surrounding the pond—the garter snakes, milk snakes, hog-nosed snakes, black racers, and pilot blacksnakes, among others—were still deep underground in dens on the hillside. Many were wedged in crevices and were curled up together in tunnels deep below rock ledges. The air temperature had not yet reached a high enough level to bring the snakes out. It would take hot days in late May and June to warm up the earth to a depth that would stir the snakes to move upward to greet the spring and summer.

But the common water snake, the dingy-brown snake so often mistaken for a "water moccasin," lay coiled on a flat rock on the south side of the small island where the young gosling had been hatched several weeks ago. Temperatures between 78 and 85 degrees Fahrenheit are the most comfortable for reptiles as well as amphibians. The snake had crawled up from a few feet below the pile of rocks on the island a few days before, when the warmth had finally penetrated to its den. It had come out of the den, in which it had

spent the winter alone, hungry. It did not take it long, with its highly developed sense of smell, to find a green frog basking in the noon sun a few yards down the shore of the pond. A quick coil, a strike, and the frog was held fast by the snake's fangs. The snake then unhinged its jawbones, which allowed it to open its mouth wider than the width of the frog, and, turning the amphibian around, began to swallow it. The process lasted perhaps twenty minutes; after that, the strong stomach acids of the snake began to dissolve the frog. That meal had been enough to stop the hunger pangs caused by the winter hibernation, and the snake was now only mildly interested in the occasional splash of a sunfish close to its rock or the sudden commotion down the shore caused by a frog leaping for a flying insect.

The water snake's vision and sense of smell were not acute enough for it to be aware of a huge shape floating on the surface of the water more than 30 feet from the island. At first glance the rough surface of the object appeared to be the bark of a floating log. It was the shell, or carapace, of a giant snapping turtle basking in the luxury of the spring sunlight after months in the frigid isolation of hibernation in the mud of the lake bottom. The big turtle, evil-looking and primordial, was floating without movement. Its body was at least 24 inches in diameter and it weighed close to 40 pounds. The three blunt keels found in younger turtles at the base of the shell were quite smooth in this old turtle. It floated immobile in the warm surface water—

Bursting Forth

61

the undersurface of the tail covered with large shields and the four extensively webbed feet, with huge coarse nails, dangling beneath the undershell.

The big turtle moved in slow motion. Every few minutes it would raise its ponderous head slowly above water to survey the surface of the pond. In its long years of existence it had learned it had only one enemy: man. It had been shot at a number of times without injury, but the sudden "splat" of a bullet ricocheting off its shell startled it into immediate action. It had been snared once with a loop and had bitten through the nylon rope holding a leg. It had been hooked in the beak by a No. 2 cod hook fastened to a plastic bottle which it had towed around the pond for four days. It had broken the length of 80-pound monofilament a day before the turtle trapper came back to the pond to locate his next candidate for turtle steak and soup. Now it no longer took any chances.

After carefully studying the pond shore for a matter of minutes, it again lowered its heavy head just below the surface of the water and slowly opened its mouth. The inside of the cavernous mouth was white. Small fish cruising near the turtle were attracted by the strange white object. They would approach to within a few inches to investigate. The head of the big turtle would shoot forward on the sinewy neck at an incredible speed, and the fish would disappear down the huge maw.

It took a great many fish to satisfy the appetite of the monster turtle, which had emerged from hibernation less than a week ago. Its first meal had been an eight-day-old Canada goose gosling, which disappeared from the line of swimming goslings behind the two adult birds without so much as a sound. A swirl in the water was the only sign that something had been beneath it in the murky water of the shallows. Neither adult goose realized the young bird was missing—then or later.

A number of other goslings were due to be eaten in the weeks to come, and none would ever grow too big to be a victim of the big turtle. One gander that came back to the lake each year to mate and raise young had a leg missing just below the knee joint. That had been the work of the snapping turtle three years ago. The battle had been monumental—the full-grown goose battling against being pulled beneath the surface and drowned, and the heavy turtle determined to pull it under. Something had to give. The leg had parted in the mighty jaws, and the goose had lived. But the goose took longer to take off in flight than its fellows, and it lay down more than it stood up.

Not only young geese would be serving as fare for the turtle during the spring and summer. Young ducks, young and full-grown muskrat, bullfrogs, mink, young raccoons, and skunks drinking from the lake, all would eventually fall prey to the huge and ancient reptile—no differently than big game had succumbed to its giant cousins, the crocodiles, for millions of years.

Three
Summer

9

Movement and Migration

June 15 near the pond saw the entire area at the peak of its activity. Most of the warblers had gone through on their way north to nest—the bits of brilliant color filtering through the forest like a huge handful of bright confetti being driven by a wind. From the fairly drab vireos to the startling black and crimson of the redstart, they had poured through for more than a week.

Many of the larger local birds—robins, cardinals, orioles, red-winged blackbirds, and woodpeckers—had nested; some had already hatched chicks. The woods and swamp were filled with flying birds searching for food; insects abounded as they emerged from larvae forms, swarmed in mating clouds, and served as food for practically everything that flew, crouched, or swam. The surface of the forest floor was the scene of great activity as gray squirrels, red squirrels, field mice, voles, moles, chipmunks, raccoons, skunks, and the ground-feeding birds dug in the damp leaves for insects, seeds, and nuts. Many of the small game animals already had young venturing outside the dens and learning from the adults what to eat and how to catch or dig for it.

Around the lake the frogs—the mating season over

—had become quiet and were busy waiting for unwary insects to show up. Their diet would consist of insects, salamanders, tiny frogs, and small fish. The bigger bullfrogs were not particular what they ate. Occasionally a larger one would pounce upon an unsuspecting young chipmunk or squirrel as it approached the bank to drink. They also had fed upon newly hatched ducklings—the pair of wood ducks having lost two of its brood of thirteen to bullfrogs and another two to snapping turtles. The remaining nine were beginning to grow flight feathers; it would be only a matter of weeks before they could leave the water and fly about the pond with the adults.

A commotion near the southern edge of the pond caused a sudden silence to fall as birds and small animals in the area ceased their calling at the shrill cries coming from the thick grass near where the small creek entered the pond. A pilot blacksnake had captured a young muskrat that had been dozing in the sunlight with other members of the brood while the female had been digging lily bulbs for them. The female had slapped the surface of the water with her rubberlike tail as a warning signal, and the rest of her young had slipped quickly into the water. Two other muskrat down the shore also slapped the water with their tails, and no water rats could be seen on the surface of the pond or on the shore. The cries of the young muskrat died quickly as the four-foot-long blacksnake whipped its coils around the small, furred body and killed it by a rapid series of constrictions. It would wait until it was certain the small animal was dead, then it would unhinge the jawbones at the rear of its head and slowly swallow its prey.

At the cessation of the cries, birds again began their chorus and small mammals went back to their foraging.

Death was no stranger to them, but merely a fact of life. All of nature's creatures are hunters, constantly searching for food, no matter what it consists of.

In a grove of softwood trees to the north of the dam, on a small flat area just above the swamp and hidden from sight, lay a tiny white-tailed deer fawn that had been born only a few moments before—the doe unknowingly balancing life there against death at the upper end of the pond. The still-wet fawn had been licked clean by the doe, which had also eaten the afterbirth. This is probably done by deer as protection against predators finding a fawn soon after birth. However, it would have been foolish for any of the predators living near the pond—the biggest being the male red fox—to try and kill the young deer. The fawn weighed only four pounds, but the doe was well equipped with razor-edged front hooves and would savagely defend her new offspring against predators far bigger than a fox by rising on her hind feet and jabbing like a boxer at the intruder.

After cleaning her offspring, the doe lay down beside the spotted fawn and allowed it to nuzzle up to her and feed until it had gained enough strength to rise to its wobbly legs. Fawns need less than half an hour before they have become strong enough to stand. The doe will then lead it away from the place of birth to a more secluded spot deep in the thickets.

Millions of years of instinct tell the doe what to do when the fawn is in its first days of life. Unlike most wild creatures, which carefully stand guard over newly born or newly hatched young, the doe will move away —as much as several hundred yards occasionally—and will leave the fawn to lie quietly alone and hidden. The fawn gives off almost no odor at this stage of its life, while the doe does; thus, as long as the fawn lies still, its spotted coat will make it almost invisible against a leafy background. The doe will return to her hidden fawn about half a dozen times a day to nurse it. This particular doe had given birth to only one fawn, while several other does had given birth to twins in the past week. Still other does in the herd—scattered about in the approximately 300-acre area—had not birthed yet and were spread throughout the thickets, eating heavily until the time came to drop their fawns.

Most of the does had been bred in the rut, or mating season, back in mid- to late November. Since the average gestation for white-tailed deer is 201 days, most fawns were being born now. But a few of the does were not bred when they first came into heat, which lasts about thirty hours; these does were bred in the next heat period, about a month later. Thus, some of the tiny fawns would not be born until July or later and would continue to show their spotted coat well into the fall months.

It will be only about three weeks before the spotted fawn is able to follow the female while she browses on buds and plants. Although it will not be able to run as fast as the adult or clear obstacles, at one month of age the fawn will be able to outrun a man. As it follows the doe on her daily feeding, the fawn will drink less milk each week and eat more vegetation, until it is finally weaned of a milk diet. This fawn is a young doe, so it will stay with the adult female throughout the winter. At times, especially during the mating season, it will be separated for periods of days from the adult doe because the doe, pursued by rutting bucks, will have no time for her offspring. About half the doe fawns born this month will mate with bucks in the coming rut. It is possible that this fawn will breed in the fall and give birth to a fawn in a year's time. Buck fawns do not stay with the adult female after the fall months arrive, but they do not breed until their second year of growth.

And so the tiny fawn lay curled up in its leafy bed, making no sound and giving off no odor. She passed her time sleeping or staring curiously at insects and small mammals that either alighted upon her or came close.

At one point she raised her head and stared intently at a disturbance only a few feet away from her nose in the damp leaves. A shower of earth suddenly erupted and a large leaf was pushed back as a tiny wood mouse burst out and scurried for the safety of nearby roots. It was closely pursued by a tiny creature not quite two inches long and weighing less than half an ounce. Its body was furred and the color a brownish gray. As it scampered across the trail left by the wood mouse, its tiny beady eyes glittered in the halflight beneath the trees. The fawn's eyes followed the tiny creature until it disappeared into the mass of roots after the mouse. Only a sudden faint squeak from deep in the roots told of the fate of the wood mouse upon being caught by a masked shrew—one of the commonest of a large clan of highly active and carnivorous little rodents that consume more than their own weight each day in food. While most of its prey consists of insects, it nevertheless kills mice, voles, and occasionally other shrews in its constant and ferocious quest for food.

Nor did the fawn miss any woodland sounds with her large and sensitive ears, so thin that blood vessels could be seen through them. At the moment she had tilted her head slightly upward to direct her mobile ears to a high-pitched screaming sound that came from the sky high above the pond. The call sounded like a long, drawn-out "*tsreeeeee—*" and was repeated several times as a big male red-tailed hawk drifted in a wide circle high over the pond. Its ultra-keen eyes had spotted another of the big, slow-flying buteo hawks, a red-shouldered hawk, approaching its territory, and it was sounding a warning call. The red-shouldered hawk, a lone immature male slightly smaller than its challenging cousin, had no territory to defend because it had not yet mated or nested. It veered off suddenly at the sound of the call and headed southwest toward open country.

The red-tailed hawk's mate, slightly larger than the male, heard the call as she sat perched on the branch of a dead tree on the hillside above the pond. The pair had been nesting in the area below the east ridge for three years now and had successfully raised a brood of young each year.

This year's young were perched on the edge of a bulky nest in the fork of a tall oak tree not far from the jumble of rocks where the foxes had their den. Two young stood on the edge of the thick nest flapping their wings for exercise while another, slightly larger, young bird was doing the same several yards out from the nest on a thick branch. The stripped carcass of a red squirrel remained on the edge of the nest—a number of flies buzzing about it. The largest of the young was due to make its first flight. The other two would not be ready for another week. All three birds were born within a few days of each other—the oldest was forty-five days old today.

The adults had mated on April 1, after several days of aerial courtship high over the tall trees of the hillside. They mated several times in the week that followed, then began gathering new green sticks for the nest they had used the year before. An even earlier nest, from the year before last, had been appropriated by a pair of great horned owls. The owls, because they

breed and lay eggs so much earlier in the spring than hawks do, have a choice each year of the big hawk nests. Owls seldom bother to build their own nests, and few hawks will challenge the huge owls' right to a nesting place—especially since the young owls are usually already hatched by the time the hawks begin nesting. The owls' nest was only slightly more than 100 yards farther up the ridge from that of the red-tailed hawks. Their young owls were fully feathered now, had left the nest, and were already expert killers on their own. By an age-old instinctive agreement, there was seldom any conflict between the big hawks and the owls. The owls could easily kill the young red-tails at night, and perhaps even attack the adults. But the owls somehow knew that the hawks could do the same to their young, and possibly even to themselves in the daylight. Both species of birds of prey had formidable talons, and though the owls were a bit stronger, it would be a fearsome contest. So they existed close together in relative harmony. Another reason for this may have been that at this time of the year food was plentiful, and there was no need to challenge a dangerous adversary.

The young hawks were hungry again, but they were hungry most of the time. In the first days of May after the chicks had hatched, the adults had been forced to tear the game they brought to the nest into small pieces; now they simply left the carcasses whole on the nest. The young hawks at first had fallen flat, wings fluttering, and with plaintive peeping calls when the adults had brought game to the nest, begged for food. Then the male, which had done almost all the hunting since the female had begun incubating the eggs, had turned over the mouse, chipmunk, squirrel, or game bird to the female. She, in turn, had fed the chicks. But as they grew in size and appetite—requiring nearly their own weight each day in food—the young hawks had also grown in aggressiveness. The white down of the chicks was gradually replaced with a thicker coat of mottled brown and white feathers interspersed with splotches of pin feathers. The young grew rapidly until the female no longer stayed with them on the nest.

Of the original four white mottled eggs that had hatched, only three young had survived. The last bird to hatch was considerably smaller than the oldest and a week younger. As a result, when food was offered, the older chicks usually forced their way to the female first, taking the major share of the food. The adults, as is the way with many birds of prey, made no attempt to select which young received the most food. The smallest chick gradually received less and less food as its fellow chicks took more and grew stronger. The stronger they grew, the easier it was for them to snatch food away from the smallest. Finally, the stunted and weak young red-tail died of malnutrition. For several days the body remained in the nest; then the adult female ripped it into small pieces, fed most of it to the remaining chicks, and ate the rest herself. Nature has an absolute and final way of guaranteeing that only the strong of a litter or brood survive to pass on the genes of the species.

The male red-tail seldom landed on the nest. It usually brought in its kill and, if the female was not there to snatch it away from him and drop it on the nest, placed it at the edge of the nest and went back for more food.

The hunting and killing cycle of the big hawks was now at its peak. Adults and young birds required tremendous amounts of food each day. Fortunately for the hawks, the region was filled with the young of all species of wildlife, from small mammals to frogs, snakes, and birds. The big hawks also killed a great many insects, grasshoppers to big water beetles, though they ate most of these themselves rather than bring them back to the nest. The young consumed gray squirrels, red squirrels, chipmunks, muskrat, mice by the hundreds, green frogs, leopard frogs, pickerel frogs, and bullfrogs. In addition, the adults brought in black racers, pilot blacksnakes, water snakes by the dozens, garter snakes, milk snakes, hog-nosed snakes, and three copperheads. In the past few weeks the male had captured two young ruffed grouse, a number of redwing blackbirds, and one young mallard duck. But by far the

bulk of the hawk's diet had been field mice, frogs, and small rodents such as squirrels and chipmunks.

Now, when food was brought to the nest, the young no longer begged for it. As soon as it was dropped on the nest the strongest snatched it and, covering it with its wings, moved quickly away from its mates to devour the food alone. In addition to covering the food with its wings it would glare defiantly at both the other young and the adults. Independence had replaced the dependency of those first weeks after being hatched. The adults simply reacted to the behavior of the young hawks—constantly bringing food and making no effort to feed the young or tear up the food.

There was a slight breeze blowing as the three young hawks continued to beat their wings—readying themselves for flight. The female continued to perch in the shade on the limb of the dead tree. The male, slowing its lazy spiral over the hillside, suddenly half-closed its huge wings and started a long, steep glide toward the shore of the pond near the dam. Its glide was perfect, and at the end it snatched a two-foot-long water snake off a flat stone where it had been sunning itself. The snake had been grasped by one taloned foot in the center of the back. As the hawk bore it to earth close to the stone, it reached out with the other set of talons and grasped the snake behind the head. Not waiting for the snake's struggles to cease, it reached down and cleanly snipped off the head of the writhing snake with its sharp beak. Then, carrying its twisting burden, it beat upward into the air and flew up the hillside to the nest. There it deposited the snake on the nest, where it was immediately grasped by the two smaller hawks and a wrestling match began for possession of the meal.

Suddenly, in the midst of the brawl, the largest of the young hawks, feeling a sudden gust of wind, took to the air and began flapping its wings wildly as it flew down the slope between the trees. It managed to cover several hundred yards in ungainly flight before it crashed through a canopy of leaves and branches and came to rest awkwardly on the limb of a large beech tree. There it shook itself, rearranging the feathers battered in its first flight, and glared at the surrounding woods.

The young hawk would remain there for a day, and the adults would bring it food. Not for three days would it be able to fly well enough to return to the nest, where it would sally forth each day for the next few weeks on its own flights. The other two young were to make the same awkward flights within a few days, and the adults would be forced to kill as much as always to keep them sustained.

It would be weeks before all three were able to fly with the adults over the pond and the hillside—and even then they would fly with nowhere near the confidence of the big hawks.

The adults would have no difficulty in teaching the young to hunt and kill. Deeply ingrained in the young hawks was the instinct and knowledge of how to do both. They would simply watch the adults as they killed. And as the first fall days arrived, they would set out on the fall migration. Many days they would go hungry because they lacked the skill to kill as efficiently as the adults. Many glides and dives would end up unsuccessfully. More than half the young hawks hatched each year die of starvation and accident during their first fall migration.

But the ones that survive, as these three young flying over the pond and the slopes below the ridge today might, would be the strongest. They would carry on the genetic strain of the red-tailed hawk.

Life and Death

B y the first week in July the young of almost everything in or near the pond was either being taught to fare for itself or already had become independent. The dependency ratio seems to have much to do with the development of intelligence in wild creatures. While the tadpoles of frogs had lost their tails and grown legs in a matter of weeks earlier in the spring, the young kits of the red fox, now three months of age, were still learning how to hunt with the adults.

When the water snake gave birth to thirty young, live snakes—it is one of the snakes that gives birth to live young while other species lay eggs—the young snakes swam off into the pond weeds immediately after birth. Only six or seven inches long, they were already able to fend for themselves.

The young of the Canada geese—fully feathered now and looking much like the adult female—were still partially dependent upon the adults even though they had learned to take off, fly about above the pond, and return. The close family bond of the geese would keep them together even through the fall migration.

The fry of the yellow perch, bass, and sunfish had long been foraging for themselves. The only fish species

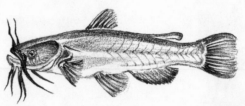

in the pond that had guarded the young for any appreciable length of time after they had hatched from eggs was the black bullhead. This small member of the catfish family lived on the bottom of the pond where it foraged all year, seldom coming near the surface. However, when its eggs had hatched in May the male bullhead had guarded the tiny black catfish fry for weeks until they were large enough to find shelter in the aquatic weeds. The male had formed the young into a round mass about the size of a softball and had constantly swum around it, keeping away all predators, while the young had churned about in the mass like tiny parts of a swirling smoke cloud.

The seven young kits of the red fox family, born about the first of April beneath the pile of boulders up on the hillside, were the survivors of eight original kits. One had been taken by the female great horned owl as the brood played outside the entrance of the den the early evening of May 16. The rest had learned a valuable lesson that day about winged predators.

They had come a long way in appearance from when they were born, dark brown and not weighing more than three ounces each. Their eyes had not opened until they were ten days old, and they had remained curled up and feeding on mother's milk for more than a month before they began to poke their noses out of the den in curiosity. It had been another two weeks before they had been allowed to play outside the den in the spring sunlight. It had not been the fault of the adults that the owl had taken the kit. Both adults had

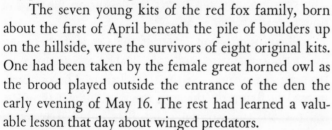

Life and Death

taught the young to reenter the den at dusk and never to venture out at night unless accompanied by the adults. The young, in their play, had simply forgotten to heed the teaching. They did so after that. Aside from the owl, the red foxes had no other natural enemies to fear—except dogs and man.

Today the adults, sleek again after having shed their shaggy winter coats, were giving the young lessons in catching mice, moles, voles, young rabbits, or any rodent that they happened to scent. They had just found the nest of a family of muskrats in which the female was nursing her second brood of the summer. The delicious aroma of warm live creatures had wafted up from a hole in the bank, and both adult foxes, after furiously digging damp dirt into the air, had unearthed the nest. The young foxes had sat quietly in a circle watching the entire excavation and joined in only when the adults tossed them the limp bodies of the young rats. The young would not forget the lesson on where and how to feed on water rats.

Their next lesson came at the head of the pond when the female fox suddenly flushed a ruffed grouse from its concealment in the thick brush. The big bird, instead of flying off through the trees after a thundering takeoff as it normally did, flew only a few yards and then proceeded to flutter across the forest floor, dragging one wing and emitting soft cries. The kits immediately took off after it on a dead run, stumbling over one other in their haste to be in on the kill. To their surprise and frustration, the female grouse kept just out of their reach until she had led them up the hillside and over the top of the ridge. She seemed to skim the ground for a dozen yards just as a young fox was about to pounce on her. When she had them far from where she had been flushed, she suddenly took to the wing, whipped in full flight down the slope, and curving around a saddle in the ridge sped back to where she had left her brood of nine. The young grouse were growing feathers but were not quite at the flying stage.

When the grouse reached the spot where she had left her young, she suddenly veered high into the air as the male fox made a leap for her from his concealment in the brush. Neither he nor the female fox had been fooled by the attempt to lure them away from the young. They had nosed out and killed three of the young grouse before the other six birds had managed to slip softly away in the maze of underbrush. The foxes had not eaten the young birds but had dropped them in a heap in an open spot. The male fox called the kits back with several short yelps. The young straggled back, their tongues lolling out from the exertion of the chase. At another barked command they dropped to their bellies and crawled slowly to the adults, in the way that domesticated dogs act when they know they have done something wrong. After turning over the three young dead grouse with her nose, the female tore them into chunks and allowed the young to eat. Whether the kits would remember the lesson the next time they flushed a grouse with young, only time would tell.

Their next lesson took place about an hour later as they crossed a brushy patch of field on the top of the ridge just to the north of the abandoned apple orchard. A cottontail rabbit jumped from its place of hiding in some brambles. It had been feeding and was not near its burrow. The adult female fox immediately took off in an easy loping run after the rabbit, which was bounding away in a zigzag course. The male fox stopped the kits from following the female with a short barked command, which caused the young to drop to their bellies in the short grass. There they watched the male with ears cocked intently forward. After making sure there were no young rabbits hidden in the grass where the adult rabbit had been hidden, the male fox simply sat down and cocked its head in the direction in which the female had disappeared.

The experienced male knew that a rabbit's home territory is comprised of only a few acres of land. In that area the rabbit is very much at home. It knows every minute trail, rock, tree, brush, and patch of bramble in the territory. It lives in a burrow, not dug by itself but reused after having been abandoned by a woodchuck or some other burrowing animal. The male fox also knew that the rabbit does not like to take refuge in a burrow—especially when being pursued by a fox—for the fast fox is able to squeeze into confined spaces and is capable of digging the rabbit from the burrow. The fox also knew that a rabbit will always run in a circle when chased and will return quite close to the spot where it began its flight.

The big red fox every so often tilted its head and peered to its left. Its acute hearing could pick up the sounds of the chase as the female made no effort to be quiet running through brush. Suddenly the fox rose to its feet, took several quick steps to its left, and made a sudden dash as the rabbit came bounding up, feeling it was well ahead of its pursuer. The rabbit narrowly escaped being caught by the fox's first rush, but it zigged and began its flight all over again. In a few seconds the female fox appeared from the brush to the left of the small clearing and flopped on its belly close to the kits. It was breathing a bit more than usual but not panting from exertion. It had known it could not catch the cottontail on the first circle so had been content to run the first of a series of relay races until the

rabbit, in utter fear and panic, would become exhausted. The kits lay in the sunlight watching the drama.

The cottontail did not go by the exact spot the next time, but passed a few yards farther to the left. The female was almost at that spot when it arrived, and again the rabbit narrowly missed death as the fox charged. The dog fox returned to the kits and sat, its tongue lolling from its mouth, as the female loped after the streaking rabbit again. But this time the female did not abandon the chase when the rabbit returned to the starting place and the male made a dash for it. She had put on a burst of speed and when the rabbit dodged the attack by the male, she also pounced. The rabbit, finding two enemies instead of the one it thought was in pursuit, panicked. It made a wrong turn, missed a tunnel it had hoped to take, ran into some brambles and—near exhaustion—slipped, scrambled, and was caught by the female as both foxes landed upon it in unison. One short scream and the rabbit was dead. The female, picking up the limp body, walked slowly over to the kits and dropped the rabbit in front of them. At a short barked command they fell upon the rabbit while the two adult foxes stretched out in the shade to cool off after the chase. Another lesson had been given and perhaps would be remembered.

The rabbit killed was a male. If the male fox had looked thirty yards farther out into the field, closer to the orchard, he would have discovered a nest in deep grass containing eight furry rabbits almost two weeks old. The female rabbit, which had remained immobile throughout the entire chase and kill, had been concealing herself about thirty feet away from the nest since the young had been born. She did this each day during daylight hours and only returned to the nest at dark to nurse the young three or four times before morning.

The reason for the caution and concealment was because the cottontail rabbit, next to mice, is the main source of food for every conceivable species of predator —from weasels and feral cats (house cats which have gone wild) to hawks, owls, and man. Every species of owl, from the tiny screech owl, the barred owl, long-eared owl, and barn owl to the great horned owl, considers the cottontail rabbit part of its regular diet. Every hawk—from the tiny falcon sparrow hawk that kills young rabbits, through the short-winged hawks such as the sharpshinned, the cooper's, and the goshawk, to all the slow-flying buteo hawks and the marsh hawk —kills cottontails. They are a main staple of the fox, the raccoon, the mink, and the skunk, which constantly raid their nests for the young. Practically all snakes manage to kill young rabbits, and a few—such as the big pilot blacksnakes and bull snakes—are capable of swallowing adult rabbits.

As a result, the cottontail raises as many as six litters a year. It needs to, if it is to keep up with its mortality rate. The female breeds so often that within an hour or so after giving birth to one litter of young, she is bred again and gives birth to another litter in just under a month. Some of the earlier litters do not survive the cold of early spring. The cottontail will give birth as early as late February and March. The death rate from hungry predators at that time of year is very high, and cold rains often drown the young. The peak of the breeding season is in May, when young cottontails have the greatest chance of survival because of more natural cover and warmer weather.

The young rabbits just up the slope from the feeding foxes were curled up in a shallow nest in the ground that had been dug by the female. It was lined with dead grass and fur that the female had plucked from her underside, and over the nest was a cover of the same material. The young were invisible from the air, but they could be detected by the sensitive nose of a predator on the ground.

In another few days the young rabbits would be old enough to crawl from the nest and feed on grasses and plants. The young would feed early in the morning and just before dusk in the evening. At any other time they are too visible to the average predator. As it is, an owl can spot them easily at dawn and dusk.

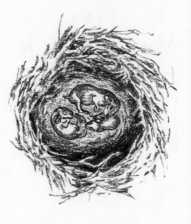

By the third week the young are weaned and are able to fend for themselves. Only an exceptionally keen hearing will tell them of the approach of enemies, and only a thorough knowledge of their home terrain will save them, for a time, from pursuit. They can expect little teaching from the adult female rabbit. She is busy getting ready for her next litter of young. It is an exceptionally lucky, strong, or experienced rabbit that lives to be more than three years old in the wild. Almost 80 percent of all the cottontail rabbits born each year are killed by predators or die of accidents and disease.

Now, as the sounds of the young kits feeding upon the male cottontail reached her clearly on the early afternoon air, the female rabbit remained so still it was almost impossible to detect her from more than a few feet away. All that showed in the matted grass was her tiny, black, unblinking eye.

The
Wood Duck

The young of almost all the small animals and birds had undergone considerable training. It was still early July, but many were already weaned and on their own. Others still had some time to go.

Far back beneath the overhanging branches of laurel bushes on the bank at the eastern end of the pond, where the water was slightly more than a foot deep and filled with water lilies, duckweed, and algae, the family of the wood duck fed in the shade. It was hot and humid weather and a thunderstorm seemed likely before too much later in the day.

The young wood ducks were almost fully feathered; although their primary feathers had not fully grown, they were capable of taking to the air. Unlike most ducks, wood-duck young do not fly early unless there is sudden danger. They had skittered across the pond in many cases and almost cleared the water. This had been caused by the attack of a mink close to the shore and again when a large water snake struck at one of the ducklings as it fed in a patch of duckweed beneath a branch upon which the big snake was draped.

But they had grown well in the sixty days or so since their hatching on May 6. The clutch of thirteen eggs had been laid by the female in a hole in the beech tree, more than 30 feet from the ground and back up the eastern slope of the pond a dozen yards from the water's edge. The female was capable of squeezing into a space three to four inches in diameter, although she looked far too big for that. The hole had once been the home of a red squirrel, but the male had fallen prey to a broadwing hawk the year before. Since then the hole had been unoccupied until the male and female wood ducks found it in April. It had been just right for the female. The big beech was at least three feet thick, and the hole was almost two feet deep and well drained. The hole was even too small for a raccoon to enter. Because of their love of duck eggs and their ability to climb, the raccoon is the most deadly predator of wood ducks. The beautifully colored male wood duck had remained on guard near the nest tree during the incubation period and until the young started pipping the eggs two days before hatching.

It is difficult to believe that young wood ducks can survive a 30-foot plunge from the nest to the ground, but it is not that impossible when one realizes the tiny ducklings are only the size of marbles when first hatched, and most of that is fluffy down. These young

ducklings floated from the nest like bits of thistle down, tumbling like a waterfall of little yellow puff-balls to the soft moss below the tree. The female had stayed in the nest during the four- to five-hour hatching process, and the brood had remained overnight in the nest. It had been early morning when they began the drop from the nest, carefully watched by the female as they landed.

They were quickly herded together for the walk through the thick underbrush to the water's edge. Reaching the water, all the young took to it as though they had been on the pond for life. Clustering around the female, they began their first trek along the edge of the bank—the female keeping them well hidden from sight. The young began eating as soon as they left the nest—the bulk of their diet being made up of over-wintering seeds, aquatic and aerial insect life, and water plants. Much of their eating in the next few weeks would be done on the shore close to the pond. The female had a fondness for acorns and other nuts in addition to aquatic plants.

Wood ducks do not dive beneath the surface as do other dabbling and puddle ducks. They merely "tip up" when feeding on the bottom and are seldom in water more than 18 inches deep while feeding. For that reason, they are seldom seen when they have a brood of young. Most of their time is spent close to the bank beneath overhanging brush and in shallow water. In addition to that, they are secretive by nature and are difficult to spot at any time of the year. Also, unlike most ordinary ducks, the wood duck is a tree-roosting duck as an adult and can and does fly into and from the tree roots at evening and morning for most of the year. But this female would remain on the surface of the pond or on the bank while her ducklings were small. They would soon learn to climb into brush and trees as they grew in size.

The male had left the female and the brood as soon as the young hatched. It was up to the female to raise the brood by herself. The male would either join a few other males or would remain hidden and solitary as it began its summer molt—during which time it cannot fly. This lack of flight feathers causes waterfowl, and particularly the wood duck, to be uneasy and highly secretive. The female would not begin her molt until she left the brood, which she would do in a short time now that they were ready to fly and had been taught all she could teach them about finding food and evading predators.

The original thirteen had dwindled to nine ducklings in the first few days of their life. Of the remaining nine, one had fallen prey to another snapping turtle, another to a marauding mink that had pounced upon the brood as it clustered about the female on the bank a few weeks ago. The third had been snatched off a branch while roosting in the midday heat just a few days ago. A male cooper's hawk, flashing out of the pines up the slope, had whipped through the tangled brush and had sunk its talons into the duckling before the rest of the brood and the female could move. The hawk bore the duckling to the ground at the water's edge as the adult and the rest of the young dove into the water beneath the bank. They had remained hidden until the hawk had carried the limp body of the duckling up to a large branch close to the trunk of a red pine far up the hillside.

Many broods of wood ducks lose more than half their number from hatching to the time they are ready for flight. Today the female seemed uneasy and restless. Her young were ready to fend for themselves, and she had already lost some of her feathers to the post-nuptial molt. It was likely she would leave her brood within a few days. They were quite capable of flight, and she felt insecure in the open where her reduced flight capabilities made her more vulnerable. She would retire to the most dense cover during her molt. The young would continue to feed and inhabit the pond until the early fall, when they would begin to congregate again with adults in preparation for the southward migration.

12

Cornucopia

The weather had been hot and humid for almost a week. It was more like August than mid-July. It had rained softly during the afternoon.

A number of species of wild creatures had already begun going into aestivation—because of the warm weather. With the first cool days of September, creatures that aestivate will resume activity, feeding and moving about vigorously until the colder weather of later fall drives them back underground and beneath water for their winter hibernation.

The hillsides and the edge of the pond, after the rain, were dotted with many small orange, lizardlike creatures. They were red efts, an inch to three inches long, and they usually appear on the forest floor after a rain. Red efts are the land phase of the red-spotted newt, which swims in the pond. There are many newts, but the most common one in the pond is the red-spotted variety. The larvae of this salamander transform into the smaller red efts, which remain as a land stage for from one to three years before returning to the water and changing into green, red-spotted aquatic adults. Few predators kill or eat newts because the skin gland secretions of the newt are toxic and are very irritating

to the mucous membranes of a predator's mouth.

The entire pond area was also ringing with the summer song of the common toad. Sounding not unlike its spring mating call, the toad—especially after a summer rain—will sing its high-pitched buzzing sound for hours on end. The sound is sometimes confused with the rasping call of cicadas or locusts. The toad is another amphibian that fears few predators, except for certain snakes. Its lumpy skin, too, contains a toxic substance that keeps away such predators as foxes, raccoons, skunks, and dogs.

The rain finally stopped. Just before dusk a female raccoon brought her five young down the slope from the eastern hillside to forage for food in the small stream entering the lake. There were four families of raccoons living on the approximately 300 acres surrounding the pond. Most lived in dens beneath rock ledges along the western slope, just beneath the ridge. This female had raised her young in a hollow tree not too far from the head of the lake.

She had bred with the big boar raccoon of her choice on February 12. She had chosen a big hickory tree as her winter den. She had found a hole far up on

the bole of the tree, a hole that had probably been used at one time by squirrels, owls, or a pileated wood-pecker. It had needed some widening, but not much. A raccoon can fit through an opening not much larger than five or six inches. After her mating, which had taken place over a number of days, the female had curled up in her warm nest, lined with bark and leaves, and had gone to sleep again to await warmer weather and the coming of her young. The male raccoon does not stay with the female after mating, and on the birth of the young the female will drive the male away from the young.

The young had been born April 14, weighing less than three ounces each, and with their eyes closed. The eyes would not open for three more weeks, but by the tenth day the little raccoons already had begun to show the marks of the black face mask and tail stripes that would make them distinctive wild creatures as adults.

A raccoon is a skilled tree climber, having a set of strong climbing claws, so it was not long before the young were old enough—at about six weeks—to crawl outside the hole and inch their way about on the main trunk. It was difficult to keep track of them, for young raccoons are as curious as older ones about everything. A young raccoon will get into trouble as easily as a kitten, and it took most of the female's time to watch them. The six young remained together as a brood until almost the first of June.

One night, while the female took the young ones on their first foraging expedition, the last young rac-coon in line as the brood crossed an opening in the light of a three-quarter moon was snatched silently away by a barred owl. Not quite as large as the great horned owl, the barred owl lacks the ear tufts of its bigger cousin. It is large enough to kill and eat small mam-

mals the size of squirrels. The female raccoon had spun about at the squeak of the young and had sprung at the attacker—giving a high growl of anger—but it was too late. On silent wings the predator had carried the little raccoon into the shadows of the night woods. The female had gathered the remaining five close to her and had herded them back to the den in the large hickory tree for the rest of the night. She did not take them out again for several days.

The five young were now three months old and fairly well able to fend for themselves, and the female was not uneasy about owls. Once summer had arrived and the young owls had scattered to other areas, the adult owls had needed to kill less, especially anything as large and formidable as an adult raccoon. Raccoons have fearful biting teeth and can inflict considerable harm even to an attacking dog. Adult males are far more than a match for almost any dog but a huge mastiff or German shepherd. The young raccoons weighed only a bit more than two pounds each now, but they had almost ceased tussling among themselves because it usually would end up in a biting match and one of the young was constantly getting badly bitten.

Tonight the female was teaching her young more about how to take food from the bed of a small stream. This lesson is of the utmost importance to the young, because in the dead of winter a stream is one of the few places where a raccoon can find food when all else is frozen over. The female had just found and cracked two freshwater mussels. The raccoon has front paws that are almost as useful as those of a human hand. The female cracked the thin shells of the mussel as the young crowded close to her, then she delicately removed the meat from the shell as she fondled it just below the surface of the stream. This habit of turning over food in water or near it has given rise to a widespread belief that raccoons wash their food before eating it. They simply have such active front paws that it seems that way. The female then passed bits of food to the young and led them into the stream with her to dig in the mud and sand of the bottom.

It was not long before the young raccoons were finding their own mussels, but it was longer before they learned how to open the shells and get the meat out. Trying to open shells with their teeth proved a waste of time.

The next item on the menu for the young raccoons was when the female caught a crayfish, about three inches long, which had been hiding beneath a small flat stone on the bottom. Before it could speed its way downstream with quick flips of its tail, the female had pounced upon it. With two quick snips of her sharp teeth, she cut off both the claws before they could do any harm to her nose or paws. A crayfish looks just like a miniature lobster, except that it is dark brown, and both claws or pincers can deliver quite a nip. The female raccoon fed on half the crustacean, then turned over the remains to the young—who squabbled about it for a few moments before each ended up with a small morsel. The next crayfish the female discovered was a little larger than the first, but instead of nipping off

the claws, she tossed the creature to the bank where the young raccoons fell upon it with enthusiasm. The enthusiasm did not last long. The crayfish fastened itself to the nose of one young raccoon, which let out a growling squeal of pain. The crayfish flew off as the young raccoon shook its head violently. The crayfish was picked up by another raccoon and got a pincer hold on the tip of a paw—with much the same results as the first time. It took at least ten minutes of patient instruction for the female to demonstrate the cutting off of the claws before any of the young would approach the crayfish with anything bordering on enthusiasm. But it wasn't long before all five had caught a few crayfish themselves.

Feeding and instruction went on for another two hours as the family moved down the creek, leaving swirls of muddy water and floating sand behind them. By the time they had reached the pond they had found and eaten more crayfish and mussels, several small water snakes and one garter snake, several green frogs, a leopard frog, and two pickerel frogs. Several water beetles had been added to the menu, as well as the young of a nest of mice found in a padded nest at the base of a bush. In addition, the female kept turning up acorns from both the water and the bank, and the young even managed to find several freshwater clams.

A raccoon will eat dead creatures killed by cars on highways; frequently it will raid garbage cans and will eat practically anything in them. Raccoons ransack birds' nests, eating not only the eggs but also the young birds. They have been known to break into muskrat dens and eat the young. In agricultural areas they wreak havoc with truck gardens—being very partial to fresh corn.

But this adult female kept her young away from

the garbage cans and the free handouts available from the houses on the hill. Her teacher had not been as wise as she was and had let her brood eat all summer from the garbage cans and food left out by well-meaning people in the homes. As a result her young, by the time the cold weather arrived and some of the people had left summer homes for the city, did not know how to fend for themselves. Two of the young in her litter had died of starvation. The young female had been very lucky that first winter. She caught just enough frogs and turtles from the bottom of the stream and in the shallow waters of the pond to keep her alive. She did not hibernate at all—being out almost every day foraging. She had learned to watch gray squirrels digging in the snow and would frighten them away and continue to dig in the spot until she found the acorn it had hidden earlier in the fall.

As the result of her narrow brush with starvation that first winter, instinct told her to teach her young to find their natural food and not to depend upon humans. Some of the other raccoons in the area did not learn that lesson until it was too late.

13

The Pond in Summer

In early August the pond, which had been gradually becoming more murky and its water more filled with algae, "turned over."

The abundance of aquatic plants growing up from the bottom had a great deal to do with the water becoming murkier. But the real reason for the cloudiness of the water and the presence of a great deal of green algae and duckweed in the shallows was the heating of the sun's rays. The pond, in spite of being fairly deep at its upper end, where the small stream entered, and in the center where it was spring fed, heated up fairly quickly in the summer. The color of the water was dark at all times of the year because water flowing in from the stream carried colors from bark and dead vegetation. This dark-colored water more easily absorbed the heat from the sun than would a pond of more clear water. In addition, in many shallow areas of the pond the water was not more than three or four feet deep. A thick silt bottom, which was very rich, made it possible for aquatic plants such as water lilies and chainweed to grow up from the bottom. In the coves and along the shoreline the algae and duckweed grew so thick it entirely covered the surface of the water.

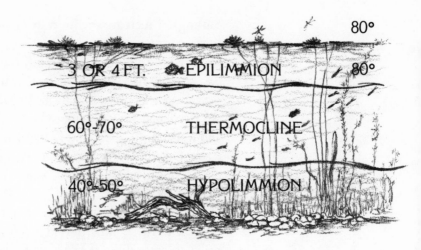

80°

3 OR 4 FT.   EPILIMMION   80°

60°-70°   THERMOCLINE

40°-50°   HYPOLIMMION

The surface temperature now, by late afternoon of a clear and hot day, could be as high as 85 degrees Fahrenheit in shallow spots. And on the surface—even in the center of the lake—the temperature could reach 80 degrees. This layer of warm water, which in a pond this size seldom reached a thickness of more than four feet, is known as the *epilimmion*. Below that warm layer there is another layer of water with temperatures generally in the high 60's to low 70's, called the *thermocline*. Below that is the coldest layer of all in the pond: the *hypolimmion*. It extends to the bottom, and depending upon the depth of the pond, its temperature could drop down to the high 40's or mid-50's. It is to the thermocline, the middle layer, that the many fish congregate in the hot weather, venturing up in the evening to feed upon smaller fish in the shallows only after the surface temperature has dropped a few degrees.

The heated top layer of water, however, can be moved about by a number of forces. High winds, such as those that accompany a thundershower, may push the surface water to one side of the pond, actually

The Pond in Summer

causing an increase in the water depth at the leeward shore. Since water tends to seek its own level, colder water from the thermocline, and the even colder layer below that, rises to the surface, bringing with it nutrients such as phosphorous and nitrogen. These foods are circulated into the upper layer of water for insects and fish to feed upon, and at the same time the warmer water is forced to circulate downward, where it supplies oxygen to the deeper water that may have lost much of its own.

Sudden and heavy rains also may dump colder water into the pond from all sides of the bowl-shaped valley surrounding it, and that water, being colder than the heated water on top, will push the warmer water down and more circulation will take place. All this tends to "muddy up" the pond toward the end of summer. An additional turnover will take place in September when the first cold nights arrive and the water sinks to its own density level as it cools at the surface. This, in turn, will cause the bottom layer eventually to reach its maximum density and the lake will slowly circulate again, bringing more nutrients to the surface and more oxygen to the depths.

Nature has a plan in all this. If it were not for a constant circulation of a pond from spring to fall, cold water would remain on the bottom all year. When the winter arrived it would cause the lake to freeze from the bottom up. If this took place here, the lake would eventually freeze solid; even the heat of the summer sun would not melt it all the way to the bottom. As a result, no plants could grow at the bottom, and no oxygen would be supplied. Fish would die of what is called *winterkill*—a situation that takes place in high mountain lakes in very cold winters. Large lakes freeze later than small bodies of water such as the pond because they retain more heat in a greater area for a longer period of time.

Fish in the pond do not generally move down to the coldest layer of water on the bottom because it usually does not contain as much oxygen as the thermocline. Fish require more oxygen in summer months to remain active. In ponds where there are trout, fish are usually able to survive, depending upon the species, if the temperature in the thermocline does not rise too high. Brook trout are the most susceptible to heat. They do well at temperatures around 68 degrees Fahrenheit, but a climb to anything much over 77 degrees will cause them to die. The rainbow trout is able to stand water temperatures of up to 80 degrees but prefers a lower temperature. The brown trout is the best adapter to warm water and is able to survive in water as high as 86 degrees.

In the bass family, the largemouth black bass is able to live quite happily in a few inches of water with a temperature in excess of 85 degrees; its relative, the smallmouth black bass, needs water where the temperature remains in the high 60's to 70's. It will not live in water above 80 degrees. The temperature does not seem to bother the sunfish one way or the other, nor the black bullheads. The perch seek the thermocline in the heat of summer.

Much of the activity on the pond had ceased. The waterfowl had climbed out on the banks during the heat of the day and rested in the shade. Even the snakes and turtles had either crawled into dens to keep cool or had burrowed into the mud. About the only aquatic predators about were an occasional big bullfrog, which needs a considerable amount of food to keep up its bulk, and snapping turtles, which are voracious eaters all summer. The largemouth bass, particularly the bigger and older ones, were active at dusk. They inhabited shelters beneath a fallen tree, a rock ledge, or under the lily pads a few inches from the bank. Lying in wait there, the bass savagely attacked any frog, fish, mouse, bird, or bat that came within range. The sound of their feeding could easily be heard across the pond as they charged their prey—sometimes taking mouthfuls of weeds and lily pads at the same time.

Above the pond at dusk, the sky was filled with the flight of bats and nighthawks as they consumed hordes of summer insects. The nasal twanging call of the nighthawk carried across the pond and echoed from the slopes of the hillsides. Masters of flight, the nighthawks, which are unrelated to hawks, would climb to several hundred feet and suddenly half-close their wings and plummet straight down toward the ground. When only a few feet from the treetops or the surface of the pond, they would suddenly pull out of the dizzying dive and climb rapidly back up to repeat the performance. When not doing that, they would fly in erratic dips and sudden turns as they consumed endless numbers of insects. The unusual booming noise made by these acrobatic birds was made by the air passing over the taut wing feathers as they pulled out of the dive—a sort of miniature "sonic boom" of the bird world.

The name nighthawk may have been given to these birds because of their swiftness of flight, but they bear no resemblance to hawks. The feet of the nighthawk are so poorly developed for grasping that they are almost prehensile. Instead of having a strong and sharp cutting beak, like the birds of prey, the nighthawk has almost no beak at all and its soft mouth is unusual in that it opens into a huge maw, which allows the bird to capture insects in the near-dark. Feeding time for

the nighthawk is limited to the short time before and after dusk. These birds are seldom seen during the day, for they perch lengthways on limbs and their brown and white mottled plumage makes them all but invisible against the bark. They will, however, flush from their nests in the spring. The nests are usually merely a depression in the ground—usually in open fields—where their two eggs are laid in gravel or among small stones. The eggs, white with splotches of gray, black, and purple, are very difficult to see. This bird goes by many names—among them nightjar, goatsucker, and bullbat. All are local names and all are misleading. The nighthawk is in no way related to the bat, which is a mammal—actually a flying rodent.

At the moment, bats were dipping and weaving above the treetops as they, too, consumed great quantities of flying insects. Most of those flying over the pond were little brown bats.

Fascinating creatures, bats up close look like something out of a horror movie; but they are quite harmless unless handled, in which case they can nip with tiny, incredibly sharp teeth. Bats are furred like mice and have long, wide wings made up of a membrane of skin. When not flitting about at night, eating insects, bats hang upside down in caves, old barns, or hollow trees. They usually live in colonies—all hanging by their toes—but occasionally they will simply spend the night in some shaded and cool spot after a heavy feeding.

The bat is the only mammal that truly flies. Other mammals, such as the flying squirrels, are capable of long-distance glides, utilizing a loose fold of skin that stretches from the back legs to the forelegs. But the bats actually fly. The wing is an extended hand with membranes stretching between the fingers. The thumb is free and terminates in a claw, which appears at what we would consider the elbow joint of a bird. The bat is nocturnal and flies only at night for food, although it can and will fly in the daylight if disturbed from its sleep. It has tiny, beady eyes, but it neither navigates nor hunts by sight. It is constantly sending out a series of high-level squeaks, far above the hearing range of humans. These sounds bounce off objects, much like radar, and allow the bat to search out its prey and avoid obstacles in its way. It can fly in absolute darkness; other nocturnal creatures, such as owls and flying squirrels, cannot.

Young bats are born alive and are tiny upon birth. They frequently stay with the female and cling to her furry body as she dips and swirls across the night sky in search of food. Occasionally the female will deposit her young on a branch or twig and will return to them after feeding. There are seldom more than two young born to the female little brown bat. They hibernate in the winter in much the same manner as other mammals do—hanging in clusters in caves and abandoned buildings—venturing out only when the first early spring sun warms up the atmosphere enough for them to find food.

As the darkness fell and the bats could be seen flying against the sky, a family of flying squirrels began their jumps from tree to tree halfway down the west slope of the hillside as they started their nightly foraging for food. Flying squirrels are so completely nocturnal it is difficult to learn much about them. Only an occasional glimpse can be seen of them as they glide from tree to tree to ground. They are able to glide for incredible distances and land as softly as a feather, running as soon as they hit the ground. Occasionally you may be fortunate enough to locate a nest of them

in an abandoned flicker or red squirrel hole. If the tree is whacked loudly enough, flying squirrels will sometimes panic and glide from the home tree in the daytime.

Flying squirrels are beautiful little creatures with soft fur, dreamy eyes, and a call that is a soft twittering sound. When they nest in the eaves of houses they become very accustomed to humans and can be tamed easily if no sudden moves or loud noises are made.

On moonlit nights on the slopes above the pond they flung themselves into the air from the very tops of the trees and went sailing off into the forest. When they landed on a tree they always seemed to run up, never down, ending in the topmost branches, where they hurled themselves into the air again—either for the next tree or down to the ground. They played in groups, and young flying squirrels would stay with the adults through the fall months. Later when the cold weather would force them to hibernate, they would winter together in batches up to twenty squirrels. Daily their food was seeds, nuts, birds' eggs, and some forms of meat. Later they would store winter food in a nest chamber in much the same manner as do chipmunks.

The Pond in Summer

The young of the pond family were born June 2—after a gestation period of forty days.

A flat, heavily furred tail also gives this tiny gliding rodent more control in the air; it acts as a rudder while the fold of skin acts as a wing surface. The squirrels need every bit of that flight control. Probably no creature, with the possible exception of the common field mouse, is the target of more owls than the flying squirrel. It is a tiny creature—the actual body weighing less than three ounces. At that size it is the quarry of every owl—from the great horned down through the barred, the long-eared, the barn, the ferocious little screech, and even the tiny saw whet owl. The several saw whets living near the pond were smaller than the screech owl, which is the size of a robin, yet they regularly fed on flying squirrels. In the nest, the little squirrels were in danger of being eaten by many things —from the common crow and the jay to weasels and raccoons. Like the cottontail rabbit, it is fortunate that flying squirrels are numerous as well as nocturnal. They have to be, with the number of silently marauding night predators constantly on the lookout for them.

14

Night Lights

The nights of summer are filled with the sounds of katydids and crickets, rubbing their wings to make their late summer songs. Treefrogs trill constantly, and the big bullfrogs now and then rumble in the thick algae along the pond edge.

After dark, the forest and slopes around the pond are alight with the magic of fireflies. Humans have long wondered at the tiny blinking lights that flitted through forests and across fields on summer nights. What causes the lights to blink on and off? A mating ritual? Some form of electricity?

Strange light has puzzled people for thousands of years. It is found in rotting wood in the forest near the pond and has the same chemical properties as appears in the firefly to produce this "cold light." Primitive peoples revered this light and attributed its fire to the gods. It shows up in writings as far back as the early Chinese writing of 1500 B.C.

The two fireflies found near the pond are the most common species in the mid-Atlantic region of North America. One has a greenish light; the other, which is smaller, has a yellow light. Both species deposited eggs in the ground after mating, and these eggs de-

veloped into fairly good-sized larvae—about an inch long—which fed upon almost microscopic animal life found among the roots of shrubs. Larvae are almost all somewhat on the ugly side; these have a horny brown body, curved jaws, and short antennae. They differ from other larvae because two lights glow near the tail.

The firefly eggs hatched four months after being laid, and the larvae began to feed as the cold nights of September arrived. With the first frost a firefly goes into hibernation, where it remains, deep in the soil, until spring. It will spend the next summer, too, as the larval form; not until the following spring, when it breaks through its shell, will it be transformed into the adult firefly. This flashing creature then takes to the air in search of a mate. The female deposits her eggs in the soil again, and the cycle is repeated.

On this night, as the fireflies twinkle and sparkle among the summer trees, it only matters that they are there—flashing signals for mates and other fireflies. Some scientists think the flashing is at times as much a communal gathering signal as it is a mating process. The male's light is brighter than the female's, which might correspond to the bright plumage and coloration of the males of many species in the wild.

Some fireflies will end up as food for the bats, nighthawks, and frogs in the water and in the trees, and for toads on the ground. Others will be consumed by moles and shrews and larger insects. Still others will flutter into webs spun by spiders and set to catch night-flying insects.

Four

Fall

The Waning Begins

September is the changing-over period for the wild things in and around the pond. The amphibians, the reptiles, and some of the smaller mammals come out of their caves, holes, and mud burrows now that the heat is leaving. There is a slight hint of cold in the night air, even though it is still very early fall. For the sun's rays are ever so slightly more angled from the south, and that slight angle is enough to tell nature's wild creatures that summer is over. The cold weather will soon arrive.

In the damp leaves of the forest floor the chipmunk works furiously to stock its many storage rooms with seeds, grains, and nuts. This is true as well for the gray and red squirrels. At night, the flying squirrels do the same.

The geese each day take longer flights from the pond, strengthening the wings of the young and testing adult feathers new after the molt. The flights are made for another reason too. The geese have eaten up most of the grass, plants, and sedges near the pond and in the swamp. The skunk cabbage, which was a lush field of green in May and June, has been nibbled down to brown and blackened stubs that barely pro-

trude from the mud. With the need to graze each day, the geese fly off in the morning to spend the day on grassy fields in the area. They will leave in a few weeks for the region of the Chesapeake, where they will feed on the cornfields of Maryland, Delaware, and Virginia and on the grasses and sedges of saltwater tidal areas.

A few hawks have already begun to pass through the area on this southward migration. The small sharp-shinned hawk and its bigger cousin, the cooper's hawk, appear with the first flights of songbirds. Being bird-eating hawks almost exclusively, they follow the migrations of warblers, sparrows, and the rest of the songbirds. The pigeon hawk, the small falcon that feeds primarily on songbirds, also passes through at this time. The tiny sparrow hawk follows the songbird migration, but its diet consists more of insects than birds.

A few leaves have begun to show a tinge of color

as the cool night air sends the sap from the tips of branches into the bigger limbs and toward the trunks of the trees. The first to show the autumn color are the elms and maples, which will soon be resplendent in reds, oranges, and yellows.

The forest is filled with feeding birds, many on their way south, and all eating close to their own weight each day in insects, seeds, and berries. The young crows have filled out in feathers, and although their croaking call still resembles the voice of a teen-age boy, they look much like the adults. All the crows are busy each hour of the day, whether it is feeding, investigating something, or harassing some form of life. They have been diving and swooping at a large black housecat, which was stalking mice in a field close to the thruway until spotted by the black marauders. After crouching in the grass sullenly as the crows zoomed over it, the cat finally made a dash for the thick brush at the edge of the woods—closely followed by almost a dozen cawing birds.

In the grassy fields bordering the big interstate highway the fat woodchucks feed, stuffing as much food each day into their rotund bodies as they can before the cold arrives. Completely unconcerned at the steady stream of vehicles that passes within a few feet of them, the woodchucks only occasionally raise a head to look for danger. And only a man, a dog, or a large hawk could concern them much. The teeth of an adult woodchuck are formidable weapons, and not many predators are willing to test them.

The big male woodchuck, feeding not far from where the crows had driven off the black housecat, was more than 24 inches long and weighed 11 pounds. A dark male, the tips of its hair were silver, giving it a grizzled look. Its burrow was more than 30 feet from where it fed, but it seemed unconcerned about danger. Since the surface of the big highway served to catch rainfall, the grass at the edge of the highway was higher and more lush than the grass back in the field. The big groundhog was eating within a few inches of the concrete edge of the road, so that in many cases automobile wheels passed less than a foot from its body. Yet it did not glance at the cars. It had fed in this way since the female that gave birth to it four years ago taught it how to find good grass, and it had no fear of mechanical moving objects.

In addition to eating constantly before the colder weather set in, the woodchuck had to keep gnawing on some sort of growth to prevent its incisor teeth from growing too rapidly. If not aligned or matched properly, the teeth of the woodchuck, which is a large marmot, will continue to grow if not kept worn down. They would eventually grow almost into complete circles. Many woodchucks have died when their teeth grew into their skulls and pierced their brain.

The heavy male had been chased by large dogs and attacked twice as a young animal by red-tailed hawks. But it was unlikely that hawks would attack him now. There was enough smaller food about for the big hawks; there was no need to attack such a strong animal.

Nor was there any need for the big chuck to travel very far. Not since March—when it had gone in search of a female soon after emerging from its winter hibernation—had the woodchuck been more than several hundred feet from its burrow. There had been enough food in the form of grass, shrubs, and insects close to the den. It ventured about only in the daytime, and its peak feeding time for most of the summer was early in the morning and late afternoon. Now that the cold weather was fast approaching, it fed almost all day—even giving up its favorite sunbathing. It had spent most of the June, July, and August middays doing almost exclusively that.

During those months it had remained sprawled in the hot sunlight only a foot or so from its burrow. An attacker would have to be an extremely strong predator to keep the big chuck from scrambling safely down the mouth of the den. Although the big male red fox had made a halfhearted charge at the woodchuck one day in June, it had been no contest. Though its extremely sharp teeth and lightninglike speed enable it to kill full-grown chucks, a fox usually will not attack an adult woodchuck unless it is very hungry. This red fox had gone on until it located a young woodchuck wandering close to the mouth of the adult female's den and, after a careful stalk, had killed it instead.

It is not difficult to spot the mouth of a chuck's den. Woodchucks make no effort to disguise their dens, heaping dirt into a mound near the entrance to them. The tunnel drops about four feet down from the entrance before making a turn and becoming a horizontal passageway. It may rise a bit so that in case a heavy rain falls there will be no flooding of the room where the chuck lives. In addition to the living room, a separate toilet room may be added. The big male woodchuck had several dogs attempt to dig it out of its den a few years back, so it had also built several escape tunnels. One, which slanted up to the roots of a dogwood tree, was invisible from the surface. The chuck had sealed it from the inside with enough dirt to keep out moisture and intruders, but he could dig through it quickly in case of a need to escape. To be on the safe side the chuck also dug another shaft, which opened up into the field a dozen feet from the main entrance. It was a "plunge hole" in case the main entrance suddenly was blocked by an attacker.

The big chuck had very strong digging claws and, while excavating, scraped dirt from in front of its nose, shoved it beneath and behind its body, and then, when a big enough pile formed, turned around and pushed out all the dirt with its flat forehead.

The groundhog was now eating more than a pound of food a day in order to form a layer of fat around its bulky body. It did not need to travel for water as it was able to absorb enough from the wet grass of early morning and the moisture from plants. It had already lined its bedchamber with a deep layer of grass, which would act as insulation against the cold. It would crawl into the burrow in late October. The sleeping room would be sealed off with a wall of dirt so that no cold air would penetrate it. The big male would then curl up into a chunky ball of fat and fur and slowly fall into a deep sleep. Its metabolism and heartbeat would gradually slow down until it was in deep hibernation. It would stay that way until February when, depending on the severity of the winter, it would come out to begin feeding. If the weather were reasonably warm, it would begin eating any sort of vegetation it could find—from bark to roots. It would subsist on that diet until the first green shoots of early spring began to appear. In the meantime it would have sought out a female, or perhaps several, and would have bred.

The young sired by this male in March had been born a month later. They had been blind at birth and had weighed less than an ounce each. Five young had been born to the female, and within four weeks they had already begun to crawl out of the den. Two of the five young did not survive the spring. One was killed by the male red fox and another by the large black housecat. The other three weaned themselves by late June, after learning to eat any and all vegetation they could find, and set out to find burrows of their own. Chucks are only sociable when they constitute a family; as soon as the young set out on their own, they become solitary. It took some time for the young chucks to find burrows because other groundhogs chased them from their territory whenever they approached. One finally found an abandoned burrow and began, by instinct, to repair it. The other two were forced to dig their own burrows and, again, instinct and a recollection of the burrow in which they grew up led them to dig it correctly.

The big male did not communicate with any other chucks in the area out of sociability, but it could communicate by its alarm call. The alarm call of the groundhog, which accounts for its name "whistle-pig," is a long, shrill whistle. At that sound every chuck within hearing picks up the warning and sounds one of its own. At the sound of a whistle almost all the woodchucks scurry rapidly to the mouths of their dens and perch on the mound of dirt, sitting bolt upright and trying to locate the danger. An occasional woodchuck digs its burrow at the base of a stone wall or fence post. Woodchucks are excellent climbers, and when alarmed, those chucks with holes next to a high point climb up on these vantage points to get a better look.

But if there was any danger around at the moment, the woodchucks had not spotted it. The big male continued to stuff itself at the edge of the big highway as a steady stream of cars rushed by it. Not one person in a hundred noticed the dark brown grizzled creature huddled close to the edge of the road.

The Completion

The woods about the pond were silent in the cold of late October. The kaleidoscope of color was almost over, and the ground and much of the surface of the pond—especially in shallow water near the shores—was covered with leaves. Many of them still retained traces of the brilliant hues of a few weeks ago when the entire woods had been one glory of reds, yellows, and oranges mixed with the dark green of evergreens and the brown background of bark. A slight dusting of snow had touched the leaves still remaining on the branches, and snow was still falling softly in the late afternoon.

The fall sky was a dark gray. No wind blew as the light snow fell, giving the pond and the woods a feeling of softness, as though they were shrouded and cushioned against any harsh sounds.

A thin skim of ice had formed during the night in the shallow end of the pond and a few inches out from the entire shore surrounding the water. No sun had come out today to melt it, and temperatures had hovered just below the freezing mark. The water of the pond was like the surface of a black mirror—making it difficult to see the water as it reflected each rock, brush, and leafy branch above it. The resident geese and ducks had left more than a month earlier on their southward flight. The only object on the surface of the pond was a black and gray male loon, which had spiraled down from a great height earlier in the morning to land on the dark surface with a shower of spray that had sent circles to the far reaches of the pond. The big bird was stopping for a few hours on its migration from a lake in northern New Brunswick where it had nested and spent the summer—to leave only when ice had driven it south. It would leave the pond later in the day after resting a few hours and would fly several hundred miles south during the night. It would spend tomorrow in salt water just inside the mouth of Delaware Bay. There it would dive for blackfish, porgy, and minnows close to the jetties protruding into the bay. But today it was looking for sunfish, perch, and small bass. Every few moments it would lower its head under water, where it would scan the depths for cruising fish. Upon seeing one, the loon would dive suddenly, disappearing beneath the surface as though oiled, and leaving no waves to mark where it had been. Once beneath water it would pursue its fish, using its short, powerful wings as well as its large webbed feet to drive it through the water at a great speed. When it succeeded in catching its prey it would surface again, sometimes more than 50 yards from where it had disappeared, with a fish in its mouth. The loon would then throw back its head on the long, sinewy neck and would swallow the fish with several quick upward thrusts of the head.

As the snow continued to fall silently, a big, fat gray squirrel scurried down the hole of its nesting tree and, after checking in every direction for danger, dashed across the forest floor to the base of a big hickory tree. There it scattered the dead leaves in all directions, pausing every few seconds to watch for sudden attack from a goshawk, red fox, or early-feeding great horned owl. Finally, after digging a hole four inches wide and almost eight inches long, it continued, periodically, to dig furiously. At last, at a depth of almost six inches, the squirrel found what it wanted: a big, sweet acorn from a white oak tree far up the slope. The sleek squirrel had buried the acorn in September—as it had thousands of others in the area—and it was hungry. Also it had no idea how long or how deep the snow might be when it ceased falling. It was spending the day eating well and stocking additional acorns in its leafy nest, to be on the safe side. The squirrel preferred acorns from the white oak rather than those of the red oak, which were bitter from the tannin in the bark of the tree. Red oak acorns take two years to mature and are not always abundant. The family of wood ducks that had summered on the pond had preferred red acorns, which had fallen on the bank and rolled into the water.

The big squirrel found the acorn by a combination of memory and scent, but far more by scent. Even later in the winter, when a heavy layer of snow would cover the ground, the dark earth far below would retain the pungent odor of the acorn and could be detected through the snow. Carrying the acorn in its mouth, the squirrel scurried back across the dead leaves to the base of the nest tree, then climbed rapidly up the trunk and far out on a big limb to the nest, where it secreted the acorn.

A sharp "clack" sound reverberated across the pond, causing the loon to turn its head quickly in that direction and to sink slowly into the water until just the top of its back, its neck, and its head were above the surface. When no further sound came from the direction of the hilltop, the big bird rose again in the water and continued its slow swimming.

Far up on the hill, in the abandoned apple orchard, an old buck and a younger one were locked in combat. The old buck had been pawing up dried apples from beneath the leaves when the younger white-tail had snorted and pawed the ground from the edge of some brush. The rut had been on for several weeks, and the big buck had bred twice. It had bred less than a hour before, and two does were browsing on elm twigs a few yards back in the brush above him. It was this odor of one of the does in heat that had brought the young buck up from where it had been feeding in the swamp.

The two does raised their heads and gazed unconcernedly at the young buck as it lowered its head and

horns and slowly approached the larger male. Not until it was within a few yards did the bigger buck lower his head. The clacking sound that had reached the loon on the pond below had been the sound of the two bucks locking horns. White-tail deer do not charge together as do members of the sheep family, causing much noise and repeating the charge until one or the other gives up. Instead, white-tails lock horns once, then commence a pushing-and-shoving contest. The older buck was considerably stronger than the younger, although there was a difference of only one year in age. The older animal carried five sharp and hardened forks on each side of its rack of antlers, while the younger buck had four. The neck of the bigger buck was swollen thicker, from repeated thrusts at brush and tree branches to keep the horns sharp and polished.

The shoving match did not last long. The older, bigger buck suddenly dug into the dirt with its back hooves, the muscles of its haunches knotted as it strained forward. At the same time it wrenched its neck muscles violently, twisting its antlers as it tore up yards of dirt and leaves. The younger buck was quickly forced backward, finally to its haunches, and nearly lost its balance as it was shoved into the edge of the brush. It tried several times to shove back, but the older buck's strength was too much for it and it suddenly backed off, shook its head several times, then quietly turned and began to browse on the tips of the brush. The older buck did not bother to chase it away; after shaking its rack, it too began to paw at the ground for fallen apples. The two does also went back to feeding.

The younger buck would manage to find does of his own in the days to come and would follow them through the forest until they consented to mate. Meanwhile, quiet settled again as the deer fed, occasionally

flicking an ear in the direction of small sounds reaching them.

One of the sounds came from a flock of more than a dozen pine grosbeaks feeding in a grove of conifers near the head of the pond. Several of the tawny, olive, and russet birds, about the size of robins, were feeding on the ground while the rest were busy in the stand of spruce. They were giving soft, mellow whistling calls as they fed. The ones on the ground were looking for seeds and insects while the ones above were eating spruce buds. They were migrating slowly south, but would not winter much more south than the area of the pond. The pine grosbeaks had nested in southern Nova Scotia, and because of an early and cold winter, they had started the southward migration early.

Instinct had told these birds to begin moving south, as instinct had told birds to move south millions of years before, when the great sheets of glacier ice had moved inexorably down across the North American continent from the polar regions. Was it because the memory of those long-past frozen ages remained that they obeyed the ancient urge each year? Obviously, intense cold and a shortage of food moved them south each year, but what caused them to become restless as the weather became warm and to move back to the northern nesting grounds? Was it homesickness for the place where they had been hatched? Or was it a dim remembrance of those huge glaciers—so long ago melted—that had gradually receded back to the polar areas, allowing birds to move farther north each year? There was plenty of food in the south. They had no apparent reason to move back to the far north—or did they?

The tropical and subtropical zones on both sides of the Equator held plenty of food for birds. But could that area support a mushrooming population of birds indefinitely? The food supply would give out as the population of birds became extremely dense. Nature has its own way of ensuring that there is enough space and food to go around. If the birds had not moved north, their population would have been cut down drastically by predation and disease. And so each year, as the fingers of cold receded from the bottom lands and valleys of the north, the birds returned. They not only returned at the same time each year, but many returned to the same area and some to the same nests—a miracle about which humans have wondered for centuries. It is a cycle that continues each year—within the cycle of life and the circle of creation. It is no greater a miracle in the wilderness about the pond than the circle of life and death, heat and cold, light and darkness, and the fact that what dies goes back to the earth—changing into many forms of energy—only to bring forth new life.

The late fall began to turn into winter over the woods and the pond. The loon suddenly left the surface of the water and renewed its journey south. Many of the creatures that earlier had scurried over and crawled upon the land near the pond were already locked below ground for the winter. For the seasons had come almost full circle again—as they had for millions of years and would continue to do for unknown millions more to come.

The woods fell silent as darkness fell. The snow stopped as suddenly as it had begun earlier in the afternoon. The sky cleared and the temperature dropped in the small valley. Furred sleeping creatures dug themselves deeper into their nests. Small birds, perched in the darkness, fluffed out their feathers against the cold and slept with a head beneath a wing.

And far above the woodlands and the cold waters of the small pond the distant stars shone in the black winter sky—remote, seemingly cold, hard, and far too distant from this tiny spot to have any relevancy to life here. Or did they? Whirling in great orbits and circles of their own—in galaxies within galaxies, all circling with geometrical precision—could they be reacting to the same laws that govern life here? What if nothing ever ended? What if everything—even in the vastness of the universe—returned to where it had begun?

The Completion

All books listed are in print at time of writing unless otherwise specified. * indicates that the book is available from the publisher in paperback as well as hardcover.

General

*Burt, William, H. *Field Guide to the Mammals,* ill. by Richard P. Grossenheider. 3rd edition. Peterson Field Guide Series. Boston: Houghton Mifflin Co., 1964. This excellent series began with the field guide of ornithologist Roger Tory Peterson, and was later expanded to include the writings of experts in other areas. You will find these titles listed below, in their various categories. The books are small, easy to carry, and accurate. The excellence of the *Field Guide to the Mammals* is due in great part to the writing of Professor William Burt of the University of Michigan. As a young naturalist, I first became a follower of his when he was editor of the *Journal of Mammalogy.*

Seton, Ernest Thompson. *Animal Tracks and Hunter Signs.* New York: Doubleday & Co., 1958. There are few nature lovers past the age of 40 who did not grow up reading the fine books on birds and animals by the late, great Ernest Thompson Seton (1860–1946). The famous Canadian and American naturalist was a magnificent sketch artist and painter in addition to being an accomplished scientist. This helpful book about tracks first appeared in 1925 as part of Seton's six-volume series, *Library of Pioneering and Woodcraft,* and was later reprinted as a separate book by Doubleday & Co., in 1958, by the late widow of Seton.

Seton, E. T. *Life Histories of Northern Animals*. New York: Charles Scribner's Sons, 1909, 4 vols. Unfortunately, this classic is now out of print but you may still find it on a library shelf. It is well worth searching for.

*Seton, E. T. *Wild Animals I Have Known*. Kottmeyer, William A., et al., eds. New York: McGraw-Hill Book Co., 1962. This book was my first introduction to Seton. It was first published by Scribners in 1898 and is perhaps Seton's most famous small book, introducing such memorable creatures as Lobo the Wolf, Silverspot the Crow and Redruff the Partridge. Seton wrote more than 40 books in the course of his career.

Stokes, Donald W. *A Guide to Nature in the Winter*. Boston: Little, Brown & Co., 1976. An unprepossessing and well researched book, extremely interesting and highly recommended to all young naturalists. It covers a subject not often tackled because of the physical discomforts of nature hunting in winter, and the common feeling that everything is either dead or hibernating in the winter woods. This fine book will dispel that notion.

Birds

Brown, Leslie, and Armadon, Dean. *Eagles, Hawks and Falcons of the World,* ill. New York: Hamlyn-America, 1976, 2 vols. I have been fascinated by the birds of prey since I was an assistant ornithologist at Trailside Museum, Bear Mountain, New York—a branch of the American Museum of Natural History—prior to World War II. Since that time, I have never read a book on the subject that is the equal of this magnificent two-volume set by the former Curator of Birds at the American Museum of Natural History, Dean Armadon, and his co-editor, Leslie Brown. The high cost of this set puts it beyond the reach of most home libraries, but you may find it at a good public library. Again, it is well worth the search.

Bull, John, and Farrand, John, Jr., *The Audubon Society Field Guide to North American Birds: Eastern Region*. New York: Alfred A. Knopf, 1977.

Udvardy, Miklos D. F., *The Audubon Society Field Guide to North American Birds: Western Region*. New York: Alfred A. Knopf, 1977. My friend Les Line, Editor of *Audubon* magazine, gave these books to me, and they are very good field guides indeed—fine supplements to the Peterson guides. With their special feature, color photographs instead of drawings for identification pictures, they are a priceless tool for any naturalist.

Cameron, Angus. *The Nightwatchers,* ill. by Peter Parnall. New York: Four Winds Press, 1971. Aside from the fact that the author of this book, Angus Cameron, is a personal friend of mine, I would recommend this book to all serious students as the finest book on owls that I know of. In addition, the magnificent drawings of Peter Parnall make it a treasure for the library of the naturalist.

Delacour, Jean. *The Waterfowl of the World,* ill. by Peter Scott. New York: Arco Publishing Co., 1974, 4 vols. I have had this book in my library since 1954, when it was first published by Country Life Limited, London. What makes it such a fine reference book on ducks, geese and swans, is not only the writing of Delacour, but the illustrations by Peter Scott, perhaps the greatest waterfowl painter of all time. The cost of this slipcased set is beyond the purchasing power of most young naturalists, but a good reference library should have a copy and your search will be well rewarded.

Pearson, T. Gilbert. *Birds of America,* ill. by Louis Agassiz Fuertes. Audubon Series. New York: Doubleday & Co., 1936. Now a voluminous book and an excellent reference book on birds, this work was first published as a two-volume set when I was given it as a Christmas present in 1936. It is a must for the library of all young naturalists, and a fine investment. Gilbert Pearson was ably assisted in doing this book by such great ornithologists as John Burroughs and Edward Forbush. A total of 106 color plates were done for this volume by the late, great wildlife painter Louis Agassiz Fuertes.

*Peterson, Roger Tory. *A Field Guide to the Birds.* 2nd edition. Peterson Field Guide Series. Boston: Houghton Mifflin Co., 1947. I have been reading Roger Tory Peterson's *Field Guide to the Birds* since I was a teenager. It was the first book I carried into the field, and the first in the treasurable series from Houghton Mifflin. For those interested, the text is also available on two LP's and on cassette, both issued by the publisher.

Fishes and Reptiles

*Conant, Roger. *A Field Guide to Reptiles and Amphibians of Eastern and Central North America.* 2nd edition. Peterson Field Guide Series. Boston: Houghton Mifflin Co., 1975. I first became acquainted with the world of reptiles when I read Roger Conant's fine book, *What Snake is That?* in 1939. He wrote it while Curator of Reptiles at the Philadelphia Zoological Garden.

Lagler, Karl F., Bardach, John E. and Miller, Robert R. *Ichthyology, The Study of Fishes.* 2nd edition. New York: John Wiley & Sons, 1977. The young naturalist will find it difficult to locate a better book on the subject of fishes. The text edition of an older work, now updated, it was a joint effort by three ichthyologists at the University of Michigan and says it all.

Other Titles of Interest

*Borror, Donald J., and White, Richard E. *Field Guide to the Insects of America North of Mexico.* Peterson Field Guide Series. Boston: Houghton Mifflin Co., 1970. Peterson came up with an excellent idea when he decided to include the experts in areas other than birds in his series. Young naturalists will find this small volume informative and enjoyable.

Taylor, Walter P., ed. *The Deer of North America.* Philadelphia: Stackpole Co., 1956. Not a new book, this fine scientific work was published jointly by the Stackpole Company of Harrisburg, Pa., and the Wildlife Management Institute, Washington, D.C. It became a textbook for students of wildlife management, is unfortunately hard to find, but well worth the search.

Index

John G. Samson is a well-known journalist whose career has taken him through all the major media, from foreign correspondent, staffwriter and columnist, to newspaper editor and news director for radio and television stations. In 1960 he was awarded Harvard University's coveted Nieman Fellowship in journalism. He is now Editor of *Field and Stream* magazine. He is also the author of several books on outdoor sports and nature, including *The Worlds of Ernest Thompson Seton,* published by Knopf. He has been a pond-watcher since his childhood in Westchester County, New York, and continues to watch the Chappaqua pond described in this book. He and his artist wife, Victoria Blanchard, live in New York City.